William Shakespeare's

Pericles, Prince of Tyre
In Plain and Simple English

BookCaps Study Guides
www.SwipeSpeare.com

Table of Contents:

About This Series

The "Classic Retold" series started as a way of telling classics for the modern reader—being careful to preserve the themes and integrity of the original. Whether you want to understand Shakespeare a little more or are trying to get a better grasps of the Greek classics, there is a book waiting for you!

Characters

ANTIOCHUS, king of Antioch
PERICLES, prince of Tyre
HELICANUS, ESCANES, two lords of Tyre
SIMONIDES, kIng of Pentapolis
CLEON, governor of Tarsus
LYSIMACHUS, governor of Mytilene
CERIMON, a lord of Ephesus
THALIARD, a lord of Antioch
PFIILEMON, servant to Cerimon
LEONINE, servant to Dionyza
Marshal
A Pandar
BOULT, his servant
The Daughter of Antiochus
DIONYZA, wife to Cleon
THAISA, daughter to Simonides
MARINA, daughter to Pericles and Thaisa
LYCHORIDA, nurse to Marina
A Bawd
Lords, Knights, Gentlemen, Sailors, Pirates, Fishermen, and Messengers
DIANA
    GOWER, as Chorus.

SCENE: Dispersedly in various countries.

Act 1

Prologue

Enter GOWER

Before the palace of Antioch

To sing a song that old was sung,	*Ancient Gower has risen from the ashes*
From ashes ancient Gower is come;	*to sing a song of ancient days,*
Assuming man's infirmities,	*reassuming the weak body of a man*
To glad your ear, and please your eyes.	*to bring you entertaining sights and sounds.*
It hath been sung at festivals,	*This song has been sung at festivals,*
On ember-eves and holy-ales;	*on the holy evenings and at country fairs;*
And lords and ladies in their lives	*and lords and ladies have at times*
Have read it for restoratives:	*read it to raise their spirits:*
The purchase is to make men glorious;	*the benefit is that it raises men up,*
Et bonum quo antiquius, eo melius.	*and the old things are the best.*
If you, born in these latter times,	*If you, born in these later times,*
When wit's more ripe, accept my rhymes.	*when knowledge has expanded, accept my song,*
And that to hear an old man sing	*and if it suits your desires*
May to your wishes pleasure bring	*to hear an old man sing,*
I life would wish, and that I might	*I would wish for life, so that I can*
Waste it for you, like taper-light.	*burn it up for you like a bright candle.*
This Antioch, then, Antiochus the Great	*This, then, is Antioch, which Antiochus the Great*
Built up, this city, for his chiefest seat:	*built, this city, as his principal base,*
The fairest in all Syria,	*the loveliest in all of Syria—*
I tell you what mine authors say:	*I'm telling you what the historians say.*
This king unto him took a fere,	*The king chose himself a mate,*
Who died and left a female heir,	*who died and left behind a daughter,*
So buxom, blithe, and full of face,	*cheerful, sweet tempered and beautiful*
As heaven had lent her all his grace;	*as if heaven had put all its grace into her;*
With whom the father liking took,	*the father took a liking to her,*
And her to incest did provoke:	*and persuaded her into incest.*
Bad child; worse father! to entice his own	*Bad child, worse father, to tempt his own daughter*
To evil should be done by none:	*into an evil that nobody should do.*
But custom what they did begin	*But what they started became so accepted*
Was with long use account no sin.	*through the passage of time it was no longer seen as a sin.*
The beauty of this sinful dame	*The beauty of this sinful lady*
Made many princes thither frame,	*made many princes travel there,*
To seek her as a bed-fellow,	*to ask for her as a bedfellow,*
In marriage-pleasures play-fellow:	*to join them in the pleasures of marriage;*
Which to prevent he made a law,	*to prevent this he passed a law*
To keep her still, and men in awe,	*to keep her for himself and deter others;*
That whoso ask'd her for his wife,	*it was that whoever wanted to marry her*
His riddle told not, lost his life:	*who could not solve his riddle would be killed.*

6

So for her many a wight did die,
As yon grim looks do testify.
What now ensues, to the judgment of your eye
I give, my cause who best can justify.

Exit

So many a young man died for her,
as you can see from this grisly display.
What happens next I put to your judgement;
it's up to you to say if it is believable or not.

SCENE I. Antioch. A room in the palace.

Enter ANTIOCHUS, Prince PERICLES, and followers

ANTIOCHUS
Young prince of Tyre, you have at large received

The danger of the task you undertake.

Young prince of Tyre, you have a full understanding
of the danger of the task that faces you.

PERICLES
I have, Antiochus, and, with a soul
Embolden'd with the glory of her praise,
Think death no hazard in this enterprise.

I have, Antiochus, and, with my soul
strengthened by the thought of her glory,
I am not afraid to risk death for this.

ANTIOCHUS
Bring in our daughter, clothed like a bride,
For the embracements even of Jove himself;
At whose conception, till Lucina reign'd,
Nature this dowry gave, to glad her presence,
The senate-house of planets all did sit,
To knit in her their best perfections.

Bring in my daughter, dressed as a bride,
suitable to be a bride of Jove himself:
between her conception and her birth
nature brought her under the influence
of lucky planets which gave her all their
perfection, to make her a joy to all who see her.

Music. Enter the Daughter of ANTIOCHUS

PERICLES
See where she comes, apparell'd like the spring,
Graces her subjects, and her thoughts the king
Of every virtue gives renown to men!
Her face the book of praises, where is read
Nothing but curious pleasures, as from thence
Sorrow were ever razed and testy wrath

Could never be her mild companion.
You gods that made me man, and sway in love,

That have inflamed desire in my breast
To taste the fruit of yon celestial tree,
Or die in the adventure, be my helps,
As I am son and servant to your will,
To compass such a boundless happiness!

Look how she comes, dressed like the spring,
she epitomises grace, and her thoughts contain
every virtue which gives mankind greatness!
Her face is a book of praise, where you can read
nothing but exquisite pleasures, as from there
all sorrows have been removed, and angry temper
could never sit alongside her mildness.
You gods, that made me a man, and direct my love,
who have given me a burning desire
to taste the fruit from that heavenly tree
or die in the attempt, help me,
as I am obedient and serve your desires,
to capture such an infinite happiness!

ANTIOCHUS
Prince Pericles,--

Prince Pericles—

PERICLES
That would be son to great Antiochus.

Who wants to be a son to the great Antiochus.

ANTIOCHUS

Before thee stands this fair Hesperides,
With golden fruit, but dangerous to be touch'd;
For death-like dragons here affright thee hard:

Her face, like heaven, enticeth thee to view
Her countless glory, which desert must gain;
And which, without desert, because thine eye
Presumes to reach, all thy whole heap must die.
Yon sometimes famous princes, like thyself,

Drawn by report, adventurous by desire,
Tell thee, with speechless tongues and semblance pale,

That without covering, save yon field of stars,
Here they stand martyrs, slain in Cupid's wars;
And with dead cheeks advise thee to desist
For going on death's net, whom none resist.

PERICLES

Antiochus, I thank thee, who hath taught
My frail mortality to know itself,
And by those fearful objects to prepare
This body, like to them, to what I must;
For death remember'd should be like a mirror,
Who tells us life's but breath, to trust it error.

I'll make my will then, and, as sick men do
Who know the world, see heaven, but, feeling woe,

Gripe not at earthly joys as erst they did;

So I bequeath a happy peace to you
And all good men, as every prince should do;

My riches to the earth from whence they came;
But my unspotted fire of love to you.

To the Daughter of ANTIOCHUS
Thus ready for the way of life or death,
I wait the sharpest blow, Antiochus.

ANTIOCHUS
Scorning advice, read the conclusion then:
Which read and not expounded, 'tis decreed,

In front of you is this beautiful garden,
with golden fruit, but picking it is dangerous;
there are deadly dragons guarding it against
you.
Her face, like heaven, tempts you to look at
her infinite glory, which you have to earn;
if your eye is found not to deserve the privilege
of looking, your whole body must die.
Those heads over there were once famous
Princes, like yourself,
attracted by stories, taking risks through desire,
let them tell you, with their speechless tongues
and pale faces,
that with no roof except for the starry sky,
they are here as martyrs, killed in Cupid's wars;
their dead cheeks advise you to give up
before you rush into death's trap, which nobody
can escape.

Antiochus, I thank you, for teaching
me about the frail nature of my life,
and showing me those terrible objects so I can
prepare my body for whatever comes;
we should remember at death is like a mirror,
which tells us life is just a breath, to trust it
would be wrong.
So I'll make my will and I'll be like sick men,
who although they are part of the world have a
glimpse of heaven,
and in their pain they don't hang on to earthly
joys:
and so I leave you peace and happiness
and the same to all good men, as every prince
should;
I leave my body to the earth from which it came;
[to the Princess] but I leave you the pure flame
of my love.

So, I am prepared for life or death,
do your worst, Antiochus.

If you won't take advice, then read the riddle:
if you read it and can't explain it the law is

9

As these before thee thou thyself shalt bleed.	*that you will bleed like the ones who came before you.*
Daughter Of all say'd yet, mayst thou prove prosperous!	*Of all the ones who've tried, may you be successful!*
Of all say'd yet, I wish thee happiness!	*Of all the ones who've tried, I wish you happiness!*
PERICLES Like a bold champion, I assume the lists, Nor ask advice of any other thought But faithfulness and courage.	*I take to the field like a bold knight, refusing to be influenced by anything but faithfulness and courage.*
He reads the riddle I am no viper, yet I feed On mother's flesh which did me breed. I sought a husband, in which labour I found that kindness in a father: He's father, son, and husband mild; I mother, wife, and yet his child. How they may be, and yet in two,	*I am no viper, yet I feed on the flesh of the mother who bore me. I looked for a husband, and in that task I found that kindness in a father. He is father, son, and gentle husband; I am mother, wife, but I am his child: how can they be so many when they are only two,*
As you will live, resolve it you. Sharp physic is the last: but, O you powers	*if you want to live, you'll have to explain it. That last instruction is pretty blunt: but, you powers*
That give heaven countless eyes to view men's acts,	*that give heaven infinite vision over the the acts of men:*
Why cloud they not their sights perpetually, If this be true, which makes me pale to read it?	*why do the stars go out for ever, if this is true, which makes me pale just to read it?*
Fair glass of light, I loved you, and could still,	*You beautiful lady, I loved you, and could still,*
Takes hold of the hand of the Daughter of ANTIOCHUS Were not this glorious casket stored with ill: But I must tell you, now my thoughts revolt For he's no man on whom perfections wait That, knowing sin within, will touch the gate. You are a fair viol, and your sense the strings;	*if you were not filled with such evil. But I must tell you that I am now revolted; it would be a bad man who, knowing of the sin inside, would still touch you. You are a beautiful violin, and your senses are the strings,*
Who, finger'd to make man his lawful music, Would draw heaven down, and all the gods, to hearken:	*which, if played by a man in lawful fashion, would make heaven on earth and all the gods would listen;*
But being play'd upon before your time, Hell only danceth at so harsh a chime.	*but you have been plucked before your time, and only devils would dance to such harsh music.*
Good sooth, I care not for you.	*[Turning towards the Princess] I swear, I don't care about you.*

ANTIOCHUS
Prince Pericles, touch not, upon thy life,

For that's an article within our law,
As dangerous as the rest. Your time's expired:
Either expound now, or receive your sentence.

Prince Pericles, do not touch her or you are dead,
that's another of our laws,
as deadly as the rest. Your time is up:
either give us the answer or receive your sentence.

PERICLES
Great king,
Few love to hear the sins they love to act;

'Twould braid yourself too near for me to tell it.

Who has a book of all that monarchs do,

He's more secure to keep it shut than shown:
For vice repeated is like the wandering wind.

Blows dust in other's eyes, to spread itself;
And yet the end of all is bought thus dear,
The breath is gone, and the sore eyes see clear:
To stop the air would hurt them. The blind mole casts
Copp'd hills towards heaven, to tell the earth is throng'd
By man's oppression; and the poor worm doth die for't.

Kings are earth's gods; in vice their law's

their will;
And if Jove stray, who dares say Jove doth ill?

It is enough you know; and it is fit,

What being more known grows worse, to smother it.

All love the womb that their first being bred,

Then give my tongue like leave to love my head.

Great King,
few people like to hear the sins they enjoy described;
if I answered it would be too close to the bone for you.
If anyone knows all the things that monarchs get up to,
he's safer keeping it to himself;
when such vice is described it becomes like a wind,
clouding the sight of others, so they sin too;
and yet death is dearly bought in this way,
the breath is gone, and the sore eyes see enough
to keep those clouds out of them. The blind mole
throws his mountains up to heaven, to tell them
the earth is full of man's wrongs; and the poor
worm dies for it.
Kings are the gods of Earth; they govern
themselves in their sins;
and if Jove sins, who dares to say that he's wrong?
It's enough that you know about it; and the best thing to do,
as when things are more widely known they get worse, to keep it quiet.
Everyone loves the womb that they came from,
so give my tongue permission to love my head, and stay there.

ANTIOCHUS
[Aside] Heaven, that I had thy head! he has found
the meaning:
But I will gloze with him.--Young prince of Tyre,

Though by the tenor of our strict edict,
Your exposition misinterpreting,
We might proceed to cancel of your days;

God, if only I had your head! He has solved it:
but I will try and put him off–young Prince of Tyre,
by the strict letter of our law,
as you have not given the right answer,
we could end your life;

Yet hope, succeeding from so fair a tree
As your fair self, doth tune us otherwise:
Forty days longer we do respite you;
If by which time our secret be undone,
This mercy shows we'll joy in such a son:

And until then your entertain shall be
As doth befit our honour and your worth.

but as you are such a good man we hope
that things will turn out differently:
we give you forty more days' grace;
if you can find out the answer before then,
the mercy I'm showing now shows how pleased
I'll be to have you as a son;
and until then you will be looked after
in a way suited to my position and your worth.

Exeunt all but PERICLES

PERICLES
How courtesy would seem to cover sin,
When what is done is like an hypocrite,
The which is good in nothing but in sight!
If it be true that I interpret false,
Then were it certain you were not so bad
As with foul incest to abuse your soul;
Where now you're both a father and a son,
By your untimely claspings with your child,
Which pleasure fits an husband, not a father;

And she an eater of her mother's flesh,
By the defiling of her parent's bed;
And both like serpents are, who though they feed
On sweetest flowers, yet they poison breed.
Antioch, farewell! for wisdom sees, those men
Blush not in actions blacker than the night,
Will shun no course to keep them from the light.
One sin, I know, another doth provoke;
Murder's as near to lust as flame to smoke:
Poison and treason are the hands of sin,
Ay, and the targets, to put off the shame:
Then, lest my lie be cropp'd to keep you clear,
By flight I'll shun the danger which I fear.

How manners try to hide sin,
when the hypocrite is acting,
and it's only good on the surface!
If it was true that my answer is wrong,
then it would be certain that you were not so evil
as to abuse your soul with foul incest;
in fact you are now both a father and son,
through your filthy embraces with your child,
with pleasures which should be for a husband,
not a father;
and she devours her mother's flesh,
through polluting her parent's bed;
they are both like snakes, who although they eat
the sweetest flowers, still produce poison.
Antioch, farewell! For it's clear to see
that men who do not blush at such filthy actions
will stop at nothing to stop them being exposed.
I know one sin follows on from another;
murder is as close to lust as flame is to smoke.
Poison and treason are the weapons of sin,
yes, and its shield, to protect it from shame:
so I will flee to avoid the danger I fear,
which is that you will kill me to avoid exposure.

Exit

Re-enter ANTIOCHUS

ANTIOCHUS
He hath found the meaning, for which we mean
To have his head.
He must not live to trumpet forth my infamy,
Nor tell the world Antiochus doth sin
In such a loathed manner;
And therefore instantly this prince must die:
For by his fall my honour must keep high.

He has discovered the answer, and so I intend
to have him killed.
He must not live to broadcast my disgrace,
nor tell the world that Antiochus sins
in such a revolting way;
and so this prince must die at once:
he must die for the sake of my reputation.

Who attends us there?

Enter THALIARD

THALIARD
Doth your highness call?

ANTIOCHUS
Thaliard,
You are of our chamber, and our mind partakes
Her private actions to your secrecy;
And for your faithfulness we will advance you.
Thaliard, behold, here's poison, and here's gold;

We hate the prince of Tyre, and thou must kill him:
It fits thee not to ask the reason why,
Because we bid it. Say, is it done?

THALIARD
My lord,
'Tis done.

ANTIOCHUS
Enough.

Enter a Messenger
Let your breath cool yourself, telling your haste.

Messenger
My lord, prince Pericles is fled.

Exit

ANTIOCHUS
As thou
Wilt live, fly after: and like an arrow shot
From a well-experienced archer hits the mark
His eye doth level at, so thou ne'er return
Unless thou say 'Prince Pericles is dead.'

THALIARD
My lord,
If I can get him within my pistol's length,
I'll make him sure enough: so, farewell to your highness.

ANTIOCHUS
Thaliard, adieu!

Who's that coming?

Did your Highness call me?

*Thaliard,
you are in my inner circle, and I confide
my deepest secrets to you;
you will be promoted for your loyalty.
Thaliard, look, here is poison, and here's
money;
I hate the Prince of Tyre, and you must kill him:
you don't have to ask for a reason,
that I order it should be enough. Will you do it?*

*My lord,
I will.*

Good.

*Catch your breath, your puffing shows your
haste.*

My lord, Prince Pericles has fled.

*If you
want to live, chase him down: be like an arrow
shot by an expert archer which hits the target
he aims at, do not come back
unless you can say, 'Prince Pericles is dead.'*

*My lord,
if I can get him within range,
I won't miss him: so, farewell to your Highness.*

Good luck, Thaliard!

Exit THALIARD
Till Pericles be dead,
My heart can lend no succor to my head.

Until Pericles is dead,
I can never rest easy.

Exit

SCENE II. Tyre. A room in the palace.

Enter PERICLES

PERICLES
[To Lords without] Let none disturb us.--Why should this change of thoughts,
The sad companion, dull-eyed melancholy,
Be my so used a guest as not an hour,
In the day's glorious walk, or peaceful night,
The tomb where grief should sleep, can breed me quiet?

Here pleasures court mine eyes, and mine eyes shun them,
And danger, which I fear'd, is at Antioch,
Whose aim seems far too short to hit me here:
Yet neither pleasure's art can joy my spirits,
Nor yet the other's distance comfort me.
Then it is thus: the passions of the mind,
That have their first conception by mis-dread,
Have after-nourishment and life by care;
And what was first but fear what might be done,
Grows elder now and cares it be not done.
And so with me: the great Antiochus,
'Gainst whom I am too little to contend,
Since he's so great can make his will his act,
Will think me speaking, though I swear to silence;

Nor boots it me to say I honour him.

If he suspect I may dishonour him:
And what may make him blush in being known,

He'll stop the course by which it might be known;
With hostile forces he'll o'erspread the land,
And with the ostent of war will look so huge,

Amazement shall drive courage from the state;

Our men be vanquish'd ere they do resist,
And subjects punish'd that ne'er thought offence:

Which care of them, not pity of myself,
Who am no more but as the tops of trees,
Which fence the roots they grow by and defend them,

Makes both my body pine and soul to languish,

Let me be alone.
Why has this new frame of mind,
this sad companion, this depression,
so taken me over, that there's not an hour,
during the beautiful day or peaceful night,
even in the tomb where grief should end, that I have any peace?
I see all these pleasures and I turn away from them.
The danger which I feared is in Antioch,
whose reach is surely too short to hit me here;
but the arts of pleasure cannot cheer me up,
nor does my distance from danger comfort me.
This is how it is: the torments of the mind,
which are born out of misgivings,
are fed and nurtured by worrying;
what was at first a fear of what might happen
has grown into a worry that it will happen.
That's how it is with me: the great Antiochus,
whom I am too small to fight against,
as he is so powerful he can do what he wants,
thinks that I will speak out, even if I swear I won't;
nor will it do me any good to say that I honour him,
if he suspects that I will dishonour him;
he will take steps to stop those things becoming known
which would shame him if they got out.
He'll invade the land with his hostile armies,
and with the trappings of war he will look so powerful
that astonishment will drive bravery out of the country,
our men will be beaten before they even fight,
and my people will be punished when they've done nothing wrong:
it's my worries for them, not for myself—
I'm just like the tops of trees
which protect the roots they grow from and defend them—
which makes my body ill and my soul depressed,

15

And punish that before that he would punish.

I'm being punished even before the punishment comes.

Enter HELICANUS, with other Lords

First Lord

Joy and all comfort in your sacred breast!

May happiness and ease fill your sacred heart!

Second Lord
And keep your mind, till you return to us,
Peaceful and comfortable!

And keep your mind, until you come back to us, quiet and settled!

HELICANUS
Peace, peace, and give experience tongue.
They do abuse the king that flatter him:
For flattery is the bellows blows up sin;
The thing which is flatter'd, but a spark,
To which that blast gives heat and stronger glowing;
Whereas reproof, obedient and in order,
Fits kings, as they are men, for they may err.

When Signior Sooth here does proclaim a peace,
He flatters you, makes war upon your life.
Prince, pardon me, or strike me, if you please;
I cannot be much lower than my knees.

Hush, hush, let the experienced talk. Those who flatter a king abuse him: flattery is the bellows which blow up sin; what starts out as just a spark heats up and glows stronger under the blast of flattery: whereas criticism, if it is respectful and justified, is good for kings, because they are men, and so they make mistakes. When Sir Flattery here wishes you peace, he flatters you, and so attacks your life. Prince, forgive me, or strike me, as you wish; I can't go much lower than kneeling.

PERICLES
All leave us else; but let your cares o'erlook
What shipping and what lading's in our haven,

And then return to us.

Everyone leave but him; make it your job to see what ships are in the harbour, and what their cargoes are, and then come back to us.

Exeunt Lords
Helicanus, thou
Hast moved us: what seest thou in our looks?

Helicanus, you have moved me: what can you see in my looks?

HELICANUS
An angry brow, dread lord.

An angry face, terrible lord.

PERICLES
If there be such a dart in princes' frowns,
How durst thy tongue move anger to our face?

If a prince's frowns are so deadly, how can you dare to say things which will anger me?

HELICANUS
How dare the plants look up to heaven, from whence

How can the plants dare to look up to heaven, from where

They have their nourishment?

they get their nourishment?

PERICLES
Thou know'st I have power
To take thy life from thee.

You know I have the power
to have you killed.

HELICANUS
[Kneeling]
I have ground the axe myself;
Do you but strike the blow.

I have sharpened the axe myself;
all you have to do is use it.

PERICLES
Rise, prithee, rise.
Sit down: thou art no flatterer:
I thank thee for it; and heaven forbid
That kings should let their ears hear their
faults hid!

Get up, please, get up.
Sit down: you are no flatterer:
I'm grateful for it; and heaven forbid
that kings should have their faults hidden!

Fit counsellor and servant for a prince,

You are the right sort of adviser and servant for
a prince,

Who by thy wisdom makest a prince thy servant,

you are so wise that the prince becomes your
servant;

What wouldst thou have me do?

and what do you think I should do?

HELICANUS
To bear with patience
Such griefs as you yourself do lay upon yourself.

You should suffer patiently
these sorrows you lay upon yourself.

PERICLES
Thou speak'st like a physician, Helicanus,
That minister'st a potion unto me
That thou wouldst tremble to receive thyself.
Attend me, then: I went to Antioch,
Where as thou know'st, against the face of death,
I sought the purchase of a glorious beauty.
From whence an issue I might propagate,
Are arms to princes, and bring joys to subjects.

You speak like a doctor, Helicanus,
who gives me a medicine
that you would be afraid to take yourself.
Listen to me then: I went to Antioch,
intending, as you know, to get for myself
a glorious beauty, in the face of death,
from whom I could breed my heirs,
bringing strength to a prince and joy to his
subjects.

Her face was to mine eye beyond all wonder;
The rest--hark in thine ear--as black as incest:
Which by my knowledge found, the sinful father
Seem'd not to strike, but smooth: but thou

know'st this,

Her looks were beautiful beyond belief;
the rest, listen carefully, as disgusting as incest;
when I discovered it, the sinful father
pretended not to attack but to be friendly; but
you know
that the time to fear a tyrant is when he
embraces you.

'Tis time to fear when tyrants seem to kiss.
Such fear so grew in me, I hither fled,
Under the covering of a careful night,

I became so afraid of him that I fled here,
under the blanket of a protecting night,
who seemed to be a friendly guardian; once here

Who seem'd my good protector; and, being here,

Bethought me what was past, what might succeed.
I knew him tyrannous; and tyrants' fears
Decrease not, but grow faster than the years:
And should he doubt it, as no doubt he doth,
That I should open to the listening air
How many worthy princes' bloods were shed,
To keep his bed of blackness unlaid ope,
To lop that doubt, he'll fill this land with arms,
And make pretence of wrong that I have done him:
When all, for mine, if I may call offence,
Must feel war's blow, who spares not innocence:
Which love to all, of which thyself art one,
Who now reprovest me for it,--

HELICANUS
Alas, sir!

PERICLES
Drew sleep out of mine eyes, blood from my cheeks,

Musings into my mind, with thousand doubts

How I might stop this tempest ere it came;
And finding little comfort to relieve them,
I thought it princely charity to grieve them.

HELICANUS
Well, my lord, since you have given me leave to speak,

Freely will I speak. Antiochus you fear,
And justly too, I think, you fear the tyrant,
Who either by public war or private treason
Will take away your life.
Therefore, my lord, go travel for a while,
Till that his rage and anger be forgot,
Or till the Destinies do cut his thread of life.
Your rule direct to any; if to me,

Day serves not light more faithful than I'll be.

PERICLES
. I do not doubt thy faith;
But should he wrong my liberties in my absence?

I thought of what had happened and what might happen.
I knew he was a tyrant; and tyrants' fears never lessen, but grow quicker than time.
And if he fears, as no doubt he does, that I will reveal to the world how much good princes' blood was shed to preserve the secret of his filthy bed, to ease that fear he'll gather up his armies, and pretend that I have done him some wrong; then everyone will feel the blow of war, which doesn't spare the innocent, as punishment for my offence, if you can call it an offence.
My love for all, including you, who just now reproved me for it—

Alas, sir!

Stopped me from sleeping, drained the blood from my cheeks, put my mind in a whirl, with a thousand worries as to how I could stop this storm before it broke; and as I could not think of a way to save them I thought it was fitting for a prince to grieve for them.

Well, my lord, since you have given me permission to speak, I shall speak freely. You fear Antiochus, with justification, I think, you fear the tyrant, who either with open war or private treachery will have you killed.
So, my lord, go travelling for a while, until his rage and anger are forgotten, or he dies.
Hand over your power to anybody; if you choose me, I will be as faithful as day is to light.

I don't doubt your loyalty; but what if he tries to overthrow me in my absence?

18

HELICANUS
We'll mingle our bloods together in the earth,
From whence we had our being and our birth.

Then our blood will run into the earth,
from which we came.

PERICLES
Tyre, I now look from thee then, and to Tarsus
Intend my travel, where I'll hear from thee;

Then I shall turn my back on Tyre, and I shall
journey to Tarsus, where I'll expect to hear from
you;

And by whose letters I'll dispose myself.
The care I had and have of subjects' good

I'll act according to what your letters say.
The responsibility I had, and have, for my
subjects' welfare

On thee I lay whose wisdom's strength can bear it.
I'll take thy word for faith, not ask thine oath:

I hand over to you who is wise enough to bear it.
I'll take your loyalty at your word, not ask you to
swear an oath:

Who shuns not to break one will sure crack both:

anyone who would break one would certainly
break both:

But in our orbs we'll live so round and safe,

but in our different spheres we'll be so diligent
and careful,

That time of both this truth shall ne'er convince,
Thou show'dst a subject's shine, I a true prince.

that until the end of time people will say
that you were a magnificent subject, and I was a
true prince.

Exeunt

SCENE III. Tyre. An ante-chamber in the palace.

Enter THALIARD

THALIARD
So, this is Tyre, and this the court. Here must I

kill King Pericles; and if I do it not, I am sure to
be hanged at home: 'tis dangerous. Well, I perceive

he was a wise fellow, and had good discretion, that,
being bid to ask what he would of the king, desired

he might know none of his secrets: now do I see he
had some reason for't; for if a king bid a man be a

villain, he's bound by the indenture of his oath to
be one! Hush! here come the lords of Tyre.

So, this is Tyre, and this is the court. This is where I must kill King Pericles; if I don't, I am certain to be hanged at home: it's dangerous. Well, I saw that he was a wise man, and could keep a secret; when he was asked what he wanted from the king, he said that he wanted to know none of his secrets: I see now he had a reason for it; because if a king tells a man to do evil, he's bound by the words of his oath to do it! Hush! Here come the lords of Tyre.

Enter HELICANUS and ESCANES, with other Lords of Tyre

HELICANUS
You shall not need, my fellow peers of Tyre,
Further to question me of your king's departure:

His seal'd commission, left in trust with me,
Doth speak sufficiently he's gone to travel.

You do not need, my fellow lords of Tyre, to question me any further about your king's departure: he has entrusted me with his sealed orders, and that's enough proof that he's gone travelling.

THALIARD
[Aside] How! the king gone!

What! The king has gone!

HELICANUS
If further yet you will be satisfied,
Why, as it were unlicensed of your loves,
He would depart, I'll give some light unto you.
Being at Antioch--

If you want further information as to why he would leave without your loving agreement, I'll enlighten you. When he was at Antioch—

THALIARD
[Aside] What from Antioch?

What about Antioch?

HELICANUS
Royal Antiochus--on what cause I know not--
Took some displeasure at him; at least he judged so:
And doubting lest that he had err'd or sinn'd,
To show his sorrow, he'ld correct himself;
So puts himself unto the shipman's toil,

Royal Antiochus—I don't know why— was angry with him, or at least he thought so: and fearful that he had erred or sinned he is doing a penance to show his regret; so he has taken up the life of a sailor,

With whom each minute threatens life or death.

for whom death is an ever present threat.

THALIARD
[Aside] Well, I perceive
I shall not be hang'd now, although I would;

But since he's gone, the king's ears it must please:
He 'scaped the land, to perish at the sea.
I'll present myself. Peace to the lords of Tyre!

Well, I can see
that I won't be hanged now, although I would've been;
since he's gone, the King will be pleased to hear
that he is fled the land to die at sea.
I'll introduce myself. Peace to the lords of Tyre!

HELICANUS
Lord Thaliard from Antiochus is welcome.

Lord Thaliard from Antiochus is welcome.

THALIARD
From him I come
With message unto princely Pericles;
But since my landing I have understood
Your lord has betook himself to unknown travels,

My message must return from whence it came.

I have come from him
with a message for Prince Pericles;
but since I landed here I have learnt
that your lord has taken himself off on an unknown journey,
so I must take my message back from where it came.

HELICANUS
We have no reason to desire it,
Commended to our master, not to us:
Yet, ere you shall depart, this we desire,
As friends to Antioch, we may feast in Tyre.

There's no reason for us to want it,
as it is addressed to our master, not to us:
but, before you leave, we would like
our friend from Antioch to feast in Tyre.

Exeunt

SCENE IV. Tarsus. A room in the Governor's house.

Enter CLEON, the governor of Tarsus, with DIONYZA, and others

CLEON
My Dionyza, shall we rest us here,
And by relating tales of others' griefs,
See if 'twill teach us to forget our own?

My Dionyza, shall we rest here,
and by telling stories of others' sorrows,
see if that will help us to forget our own?

DIONYZA
That were to blow at fire in hope to quench it;

For who digs hills because they do aspire
Throws down one mountain to cast up a higher.
O my distressed lord, even such our griefs are;

Here they're but felt, and seen with mischief's eyes,
But like to groves, being topp'd, they higher rise.

That would be blowing up the fire to try and put
it out;
if you try to dig up one mountain
the rubble will make another, higher.
Oh my sad lord, this is what our sorrows are
like;
at the moment they just are what they are,
but like trees, once they are pruned, they'll get
bigger.

CLEON
O Dionyza,
Who wanteth food, and will not say he wants it,
Or can conceal his hunger till he famish?
Our tongues and sorrows do sound deep
Our woes into the air; our eyes do weep,
Till tongues fetch breath that may proclaim them
louder;
That, if heaven slumber while their creatures want,

They may awake their helps to comfort them.
I'll then discourse our woes, felt several years,

And wanting breath to speak help me with tears.

Oh Dionyza,
who wants food and will not say he wants it,
or can hide his hunger until he starves?
Our tongues and sorrows broadcast
our sadness into the air; our eyes weep,
until our tongues get fresh breath to make
them louder;
so that if the gods sleep while their creatures are
in need
they can be woken to give them comfort.
So I'll talk about our sorrows, which we have
had for several years,
and if you can't speak then back me up with your
tears.

DIONYZA
I'll do my best, sir.

I'll do my best, sir.

CLEON
This Tarsus, o'er which I have the government,
A city on whom plenty held full hand,
For riches strew'd herself even in the streets;
Whose towers bore heads so high they kiss'd the
clouds,
And strangers ne'er beheld but wondered at;

This Tarsus, over which I rule,
the city that was blessed by plenty,
with streets almost paved with gold;
towers which reached so high they kissed the
clouds,
which strangers never saw without being
amazed by;

Whose men and dames so jetted and adorn'd,

Like one another's glass to trim them by:
Their tables were stored full, to glad the sight,

And not so much to feed on as delight;
All poverty was scorn'd, and pride so great,
The name of help grew odious to repeat.

DIONYZA
O, 'tis too true.

CLEON
But see what heaven can do! By this our change,

These mouths, who but of late, earth, sea, and air,

Were all too little to content and please,
Although they gave their creatures in abundance,
As houses are defiled for want of use,
They are now starved for want of exercise:
Those palates who, not yet two summers younger,
Must have inventions to delight the taste,
Would now be glad of bread, and beg for it:

Those mothers who, to nousle up their babes,

Thought nought too curious, are ready now
To eat those little darlings whom they loved.
So sharp are hunger's teeth, that man and wife
Draw lots who first shall die to lengthen life:

Here stands a lord, and there a lady weeping;

Here many sink, yet those which see them fall
Have scarce strength left to give them burial.
Is not this true?

DIONYZA
Our cheeks and hollow eyes do witness it.

CLEON
O, let those cities that of plenty's cup
And her prosperities so largely taste,
With their superfluous riots, hear these tears!
The misery of Tarsus may be theirs.

Enter a Lord

whose men and women were so haughty and decorated,
and they saw their image in all the others:
their tables were well stocked, pleasing to the eye,
and they loved the luxury more than the food;
all poverty was hated, and they were so proud,
that they would disdain to ask for help.

Alas, that's too true.

Just see what heaven can do! Since the change in fortunes,
these mouths, which only recently didn't bother to praise
the earth, sea and air, even though they gave such a great quantity of riches,
as houses become rundown through lack of use,
they are now starved through lack of use;
those mouths which less than two summers ago needed fancy foods to get them excited
would now be happy with bread and they beg for it;
those mothers who thought that nothing was too good
to feed their babies with, are now ready
to eat the little darlings that they loved.
Hunger is hitting so hard, that man and wife draw lots to see who will die first to help the other live.
Here you can see a lord, and there a lady weeping;
many are dying, but those who see them fall have hardly enough strength left to bury them.
Isn't this true?

Our cheeks and sunken eyes show it.

Oh let those cities that are prospering and who enjoy all the fruits of plenty,
with wasteful indulgence, hear these tears!
One day the fate of Tarsus might be theirs.

Lord
Where's the lord governor?

Where's the lord governor?

CLEON
Here.
Speak out thy sorrows which thou bring'st in haste,

For comfort is too far for us to expect.

Here.
Tell us the bad news which has brought you rushing here,
because we know you cannot have any good.

Lord
We have descried, upon our neighbouring shore,
A portly sail of ships make hitherward.

We have spotted, from the shore,
a great fleet of ships coming this way.

CLEON
I thought as much.
One sorrow never comes but brings an heir,
That may succeed as his inheritor;
And so in ours: some neighbouring nation,

Taking advantage of our misery,
Hath stuff'd these hollow vessels with their power,
To beat us down, the which are down already;

And make a conquest of unhappy me,
Whereas no glory's got to overcome.

I was expecting this.
Sorrows never come singly,
there is always another one following;
this is the case here: some neighbouring country,
taking advantage of our misfortune,
has loaded those ships with their forces
to beat us down, when we are on our knees already;
they want to triumph over me,
which would not bring anyone any glory.

Lord
That's the least fear; for, by the semblance
Of their white flags display'd, they bring us peace,

And come to us as favourers, not as foes.

We don't have to fear that, by the look
of the white flags they are flying, they have come in peace,
as helpers, not as enemies.

CLEON
Thou speak'st like him's untutor'd to repeat:
Who makes the fairest show means most deceit.
But bring they what they will and what they can,
What need we fear?
The ground's the lowest, and we are half way there.

Go tell their general we attend him here,

To know for what he comes, and whence he comes,

And what he craves.

You speak like an innocent:
the fairest face hides the filthiest plans.
But whatever they're bringing here,
why should we be afraid?
One can't get lower than the ground, and we are halfway there.
Go and tell their general that we are waiting for him here,
to learn why he comes, and from where he comes,
and what he wants.

Lord

24

I go, my lord.

I will go, my lord.

Exit

CLEON
Welcome is peace, if he on peace consist;
If wars, we are unable to resist.

Peace is welcome, if peace is what he intends;
if he wants war, we cannot fight him.

Enter PERICLES with Attendants

PERICLES
Lord governor, for so we hear you are,
Let not our ships and number of our men
Be like a beacon fired to amaze your eyes.
We have heard your miseries as far as Tyre,
And seen the desolation of your streets:
Nor come we to add sorrow to your tears,
But to relieve them of their heavy load;
And these our ships, you happily may think
Are like the Trojan horse was stuff'd within
With bloody veins, expecting overthrow,
Are stored with corn to make your needy bread,

And give them life whom hunger starved half dead.

Lord governor, for that's what we hear you are,
don't let our ships and the number of forces
be like a warning fire to cause you alarm.
We heard of your misery as far away as Tyre,
and have seen the desolation in your streets:
we have not come to add to your sorrows,
but to relieve them;
these ships of ours, which you probably think
are like the Trojan horse, filled with
bloodthirsty men lusting for victory,
are in fact full of corn to make the bread you
need,
and to give life to those who are almost starved
to death.

All
The gods of Greece protect you!
And we'll pray for you.

May the gods of Greece protect you!
We shall pray for you.

PERICLES
Arise, I pray you, rise:
We do not look for reverence, but to love,
And harbourage for ourself, our ships, and men.

Get up, please, get up:
we are not looking for worship but for love,
and a safe harbour for myself, my ships and my
men.

CLEON
The which when any shall not gratify,
Or pay you with unthankfulness in thought,
Be it our wives, our children, or ourselves,
The curse of heaven and men succeed their evils!

Till when,--the which I hope shall ne'er be seen,--
Your grace is welcome to our town and us.

If anyone fails to provide this for you,
or does not feel the proper gratitude they should,
whether it's our wives, our children or ourselves,
may the curses of heaven and men fall upon
them!
Until then–and I hope that will never happen–
your grace is welcome to our town, and
welcomed by us.

PERICLES
Which welcome we'll accept; feast here awhile,

We'll accept your welcome; eat with us now,

Until our stars that frown lend us a smile.   *until sadness turns to happiness.*

Exeunt

Act 2

SCENE I. Pentapolis. An open place by the sea-side.

Enter GOWER

GOWER
Here have you seen a mighty king
His child, I wis, to incest bring;
A better prince and benign lord,
That will prove awful both in deed and word

Be quiet then as men should be,
Till he hath pass'd necessity.
I'll show you those in troubles reign,
Losing a mite, a mountain gain.
The good in conversation,
To whom I give my benison,
Is still at Tarsus, where each man
Thinks all is writ he speken can;
And, to remember what he does,
Build his statue to make him glorious:

But tidings to the contrary
Are brought your eyes; what need speak I?

DUMB SHOW.

Enter at one door PERICLES talking with CLEON;
all the train with them. Enter at another door a
Gentleman, with a letter to PERICLES; PERICLES
shows the letter to CLEON; gives the Messenger a
reward, and knights him. Exit PERICLES at one
door, and CLEON at another

Good Helicane, that stay'd at home,
Not to eat honey like a drone
From others' labours; for though he strive
To killen bad, keep good alive;
And to fulfil his prince' desire,
Sends word of all that haps in Tyre:
How Thaliard came full bent with sin
And had intent to murder him;
And that in Tarsus was not best
Longer for him to make his rest.
He, doing so, put forth to seas,

*Here you have seen the mighty King
persuade his child to incest;
and a better prince and kindly lord
who will prove himself awesome in deeds and
words,
keep quiet then, as one should be
until he has survived his hardships.
I'll show you those who have troubles,
who lose a pebble and gain a mountain.
The one whose conduct is good,
whom I bless,
is still at Tarsus, where each man
thinks he has the skill to speak holy writ;
and in commemoration of himself,
builds his statue to glorify himself. But news of
other things*

*is brought before your eyes; why do I need to
speak?*

DUMB SHOW.

*Enter at one door PERICLES talking with
CLEON; all the train with them. Enter at
another door a Gentleman, with a letter to
PERICLES; PERICLES shows the letter to
CLEON; gives the Messenger a reward, and
knights him. Exit PERICLES at one door, and
CLEON at another*

*Good Helicanus has stayed home,
not to exploit the work
of others; he works
to kill the bad, to save the good;
following his prince's orders
he sends word of all that happens in Tyre:
how Thaliard came with sinful purpose
and hidden plans to murder him;
he told him that it was no longer
advisable for him to stay in Tarsus.
Hearing this he set out to sea,*

Where when men been, there's seldom ease;
For now the wind begins to blow;
Thunder above and deeps below
Make such unquiet, that the ship
Should house him safe is wreck'd and split;

And he, good prince, having all lost,
By waves from coast to coast is tost:
All perishen of man, of pelf,
Ne aught escapen but himself;
Till fortune, tired with doing bad,
Threw him ashore, to give him glad:
And here he comes. What shall be next,
Pardon old Gower,--this longs the text.

Exit

Enter PERICLES, wet

PERICLES
Yet cease your ire, you angry stars of heaven!

Wind, rain, and thunder, remember, earthly man
Is but a substance that must yield to you;
And I, as fits my nature, do obey you:
Alas, the sea hath cast me on the rocks,
Wash'd me from shore to shore, and left me breath

Nothing to think on but ensuing death:
Let it suffice the greatness of your powers
To have bereft a prince of all his fortunes;
And having thrown him from your watery grave,

Here to have death in peace is all he'll crave.

Enter three FISHERMEN

First Fisherman
What, ho, Pilch!

Second Fisherman
Ha, come and bring away the nets!

First Fisherman
What, Patch-breech, I say!

Third Fisherman
What say you, master?

which is seldom a restful place for men;
now the wind begins to blow;
thunder above and depths below
causes such disruption that the ship
which should have protected him is wrecked and sunk;
and he, good prince, having lost everything,
is tossed from coast to coast by the waves.
All the men and cargo were lost,
nobody escaped but himself;
until fate, tired with treating him badly,
cast him ashore, to make him happy:
and here he comes. As to what happens next,
excuse old Gower–you'll see from the text.

Now stop your anger, you furious stars of heaven!
Remember, wind, rain and thunder, earthly man
is only a substance that must give in to you;
as is appropriate for my nature, I obey you:
alas the sea has thrown me on the rocks,
washed me from shore to shore, and left me so breathless
all I can think of is my oncoming death:
be satisfied that your great powers
have stripped a prince of all his fortunes;
now you've thrown him out of your watery grave,
all he wants is to have a peaceful death here.

Hello there, Pilch!

Hey, bring the nets over here!

Hey there, Patch-breech, hey!

What are you saying, master?

First Fisherman
Look how thou stirrest now! come away, or I'll
fetch thee with a wanion.

Aren't you moving yet! You get a move on, or I'll give you such a smack!

Third Fisherman
Faith, master, I am thinking of the poor men that

were cast away before us even now.

*I swear, master, I am thinking of the poor men who
were shipwrecked in front of us recently.*

First Fisherman
Alas, poor souls, it grieved my heart to hear what
pitiful cries they made to us to help them, when,
well-a-day, we could scarce help ourselves.

*Alas, poor souls, it broke my heart to hear their pitiful cries for help, when, alas,
we could hardly help ourselves.*

Third Fisherman
Nay, master, said not I as much when I saw the
porpus how he bounced and tumbled? they say

they're half fish, half flesh: a plague on them,
they ne'er come but I look to be washed. Master, I

marvel how the fishes live in the sea.

*Now, master, didn't I say trouble was coming when I saw how the porpoises were jumping? They say
they're half fish, half man: damn them,
every time they appear I expect the boat to be swamped.
Master, I am amazed how the fish manage to live in the sea.*

First Fisherman
Why, as men do a-land; the great ones eat up the

little ones: I can compare our rich misers to

nothing so fitly as to a whale; a' plays and
tumbles, driving the poor fry before him, and at

last devours them all at a mouthful: such whales

have I heard on o' the land, who never leave gaping

till they've swallowed the whole parish, church,

steeple, bells, and all.

*Why, just as men do on land; the great ones eat up the
little ones: the best comparison for our rich misers
is a whale; he plays and
tumbles, driving the minnows ahead of him, and at last
swallows them all in one mouthful: I have heard of
such whales on the land, who never close their mouths
until they've swallowed the whole parish, church,
steeple, bells and all.*

PERICLES
[Aside] A pretty moral.

A nice little parable.

Third Fisherman
But, master, if I had been the sexton, I would have

been that day in the belfry.

*But, master, if I had been the church keeper, I would have
made sure I was in the belfry that day.*

Second Fisherman
Why, man?

Why, man?

Third Fisherman
Because he should have swallowed me too: and when I

had been in his belly, I would have kept such a
jangling of the bells, that he should never have
left, till he cast bells, steeple, church, and

parish up again. But if the good King Simonides
were of my mind,--

Because he would have swallowed me too: and when I
was in his belly, I would have kept up such a
racket with the bells that he would have no rest
until he had vomited up the bells, steeple, church
and
parish again. But if the good King Simonides
thought like me–

PERICLES
[Aside] Simonides!

Simonides!

Third Fisherman
We would purge the land of these drones, that rob

the bee of her honey.

We would strip the land of these drones, that
steal
the honey from the bee.

PERICLES
[Aside] How from the finny subject of the sea

These fishers tell the infirmities of men;
And from their watery empire recollect
All that may men approve or men detect!
Peace be at your labour, honest fishermen.

How well these fishermen describe the
weaknesses of men
in terms of the fish of the sea;
from their watery empire they find examples
of all the characteristics of men!
Blessings on your work, honest fishermen.

Second Fisherman
Honest! good fellow, what's that? If it be a day
fits you, search out of the calendar, and nobody
look after it.

Honest! Dear chap, what's that? If it's a day
in the year that suits you, find it on the calendar,
but nobody else will see it.

PERICLES
May see the sea hath cast upon your coast–

You may have seen that the sea has washed up
on your coast–

Second Fisherman
What a drunken knave was the sea to cast thee in our

way!

What a drunken scoundrel the sea was to throw
you
in our path!

PERICLES
A man whom both the waters and the wind,
In that vast tennis-court, have made the ball

I'm a man whom both the waters and the wind
have made their tennis ball on that enormous

31

For them to play upon, entreats you pity him:

He asks of you, that never used to beg.

First Fisherman
No, friend, cannot you beg? Here's them in our

country Greece gets more with begging than we can do

with working.

Second Fisherman
Canst thou catch any fishes, then?

PERICLES
I never practised it.

Second Fisherman
Nay, then thou wilt starve, sure; for here's nothing

to be got now-a-days, unless thou canst fish for't.

PERICLES
What I have been I have forgot to know;
But what I am, want teaches me to think on:
A man throng'd up with cold: my veins are chill,

And have no more of life than may suffice
To give my tongue that heat to ask your help;
Which if you shall refuse, when I am dead,
For that I am a man, pray see me buried.

First Fisherman
Die quoth-a? Now gods forbid! I have a gown here;

come, put it on; keep thee warm. Now, afore me, a

handsome fellow! Come, thou shalt go home, and

we'll have flesh for holidays, fish for
fasting-days, and moreo'er puddings and flap-jacks,

and thou shalt be welcome.

PERICLES
I thank you, sir.

court for them to play with, and I ask you to pity me:
I'm asking you, I never used to beg.

Really, friend, you can't beg? There are those in our
country of Greece who get more with begging than we do
from working.

Can you catch fish, then?

I've never tried.

Well then you will starve, for sure; there's nothing
else to eat in these parts, unless you fish for it.

I have forgotten what I used to be;
but my need makes me think of what I am now:
a man overwhelmed with cold: my blood is chilled
and I have only just enough energy to let me
move my tongue enough to ask you for help;
if you refuse to help me, when I'm dead,
out of humanity please see that I am buried.

Is he talking about dying? Heaven forbid! I have a gown here;
come on, put it on, keep yourself warm. Now, look at that,
a handsome fellow! Come on, you shall come home, and
we'll have meat on holidays, fish on fasting days, and what's more we'll have puddings and flapjacks,
and you will be welcome.

Thank you, sir.

32

Second Fisherman
Hark you, my friend; you said you could not beg.

Listen here, my friend; you said you could not beg.

PERICLES
I did but crave.

All I did was ask.

Second Fisherman
But crave! Then I'll turn craver too, and so I shall 'scape whipping.

Just ask! Then I'll become an asker too, and so I won't get whipped.

PERICLES
Why, are all your beggars whipped, then?

Why, do all your beggars get whipped, then?

Second Fisherman
O, not all, my friend, not all; for if all your beggars were whipped, I would wish no better office

than to be beadle. But, master, I'll go draw up the

net.

Oh, not all, my friend, not all; if all the beggars were whipped, I could wish for no better job
than to be the beadle. But, master, I'll go and pull up
the net.

Exit with Third Fisherman

PERICLES
[Aside] How well this honest mirth becomes their labour!

How well this honest humour suits their work!

First Fisherman
Hark you, sir, do you know where ye are?

Listen, sir, do you know where you are?

PERICLES
Not well.

Not exactly.

First Fisherman
Why, I'll tell you: this is called Pentapolis, and

our king the good Simonides.

Well, I'll tell you: this place is called Pentapolis, and
our king is the good Simonides.

PERICLES
The good King Simonides, do you call him?

The good King Simonides, you call him?

First Fisherman
Ay, sir; and he deserves so to be called for his peaceable reign and good government.

Yes, sir; and he deserves the name for his peaceful reign and good government.

PERICLES
He is a happy king, since he gains from his subjects

He is a lucky king, since his subjects call him

the name of good by his government. How far is his court distant from this shore?

First Fisherman
Marry, sir, half a day's journey: and I'll tell you, he hath a fair daughter, and to-morrow is her

birth-day; and there are princes and knights come from all parts of the world to just and tourney for her love.

PERICLES
Were my fortunes equal to my desires, I could wish to make one there.

First Fisherman
O, sir, things must be as they may; and what a man cannot get, he may lawfully deal for his wife's soul.

Re-enter Second and Third Fishermen, drawing up a net

Second Fisherman
Help, master, help! here's a fish hangs in the net,

like a poor man's right in the law; 'twill hardly

come out. Ha! bots on't, 'tis come at last, and

'tis turned to a rusty armour.

PERICLES
An armour, friends! I pray you, let me see it.
Thanks, fortune, yet, that, after all my crosses,
Thou givest me somewhat to repair myself;
And though it was mine own, part of my heritage,
Which my dead father did bequeath to me,
With this strict charge, even as he left his life,
'Keep it, my Pericles; it hath been a shield
Twixt me and death;'--and pointed to this brace;--

'For that it saved me, keep it; in like necessity--

The which the gods protect thee from!--may

defend thee.'
It kept where I kept, I so dearly loved it;
Till the rough seas, that spare not any man,

---

*good
on account of his government. How far is his court from this shore?*

*Well, sir, half a day's journey: and I'll you, he has a beautiful daughter, and tomorrow is her
birthday; princes and knights have come from all over the world to joust and compete for her love.*

If my fortune matched my wishes, I would wish to be one of them.

Oh sir, things go the way they will; what a man can't get he can always swap for his wife's soul.

*Help, master, help! There's a fish caught in the net,
like a poor man caught in a lawsuit; it's almost impossible
to get it out. Ha! Curse it, it's come out at last, and
it turns out to be a rusty suit of armour.*

*A suit of armour, friends! Please, let me see it.
I thank you, Fortune, that after all my setbacks you have given me a way of restoring myself;
this was my own, part of my inheritance, which my dead father left to me
with these strict instructions, even as he died,
'Keep it, my Pericles; it has been a shield between me and death;'--and he pointed to this armguard--
'because it saved me, keep it; if you're in the same trouble,
which I hope the gods keep you from, may it protect you!'*

It went with me everywhere--I loved it so dearly--until the rough sea, that doesn't spare anybody,

Took it in rage, though calm'd have given't again:

took it in its rage, although in the calm it has given it back.

I thank thee for't: my shipwreck now's no ill,

Since I have here my father's gift in's will.

Thank you for this; my shipwreck is now no hardship,
since I have here what my father left me in his will.

First Fisherman
What mean you, sir?

What do you mean, sir?

PERICLES
To beg of you, kind friends, this coat of worth,

To beg you, kind friends, to let me have this coat,

For it was sometime target to a king;
I know it by this mark. He loved me dearly,

which once upon a time shielded a king;
I recognise it from this mark. He loved me dearly,

And for his sake I wish the having of it;
And that you'ld guide me to your sovereign's court,

and I should like to have it to remember him by;
and I would like you to guide me to your king's court,

Where with it I may appear a gentleman;

where it will help me to appear like a gentleman;

And if that ever my low fortune's better,
I'll pay your bounties; till then rest your debtor.

if my fortunes ever improve
I will pay you a reward; until then I'll be in your debt.

First Fisherman
Why, wilt thou tourney for the lady?

What, will you compete for the lady?

PERICLES
I'll show the virtue I have borne in arms.

I'll show the skills I have in combat.

First Fisherman
Why, do 'e take it, and the gods give thee good on't!

Well, have it, and may you have good luck with it!

Second Fisherman
Ay, but hark you, my friend; 'twas we that made up
this garment through the rough seams of the waters:
there are certain condolements, certain vails. I
hope, sir, if you thrive, you'll remember from

whence you had it.

Yes, but listen here, my friend; it was we who pulled this garment out of the rough seas:
there should be some reward, some tip. I hope, sir, that if you do well, you will remember where
you got it from.

PERICLES
Believe 't, I will.
By your furtherance I am clothed in steel;

Believe me, I will.
With your help I am armoured in steel;

And, spite of all the rapture of the sea,
This jewel holds his building on my arm:
Unto thy value I will mount myself
Upon a courser, whose delightful steps
Shall make the gazer joy to see him tread.
Only, my friend, I yet am unprovided
Of a pair of bases.

and, in spite of all the damage of the sea,
this jewel still shines upon my arm:
I will use it to get the best horse it can
buy, whose delightful steps
will make the onlookers love to see him walk.
Except, my friends, I don't yet have
the knightly skirts.

Second Fisherman
We'll sure provide: thou shalt have my best gown to
make thee a pair; and I'll bring thee to the court myself.

We'll provide those: we shall make a pair out of
my best gown; and I'll bring you to the court
myself.

PERICLES
Then honour be but a goal to my will,
This day I'll rise, or else add ill to ill.

Then honour will be my goal,
I shall rise up, or things will get worse.

Exeunt

SCENE II. The same.

A public way or platform leading to the
lists. A pavilion by the side of it for the
reception of King, Princess, Lords, & c.

Enter SIMONIDES, THAISA, Lords, and Attendants

SIMONIDES
Are the knights ready to begin the triumph?

Are the knights ready to begin the festivities?

First Lord
They are, my liege;
And stay your coming to present themselves.

They are, my lord;
they are waiting for your arrival to present
themselves.

SIMONIDES
Return them, we are ready; and our daughter,
In honour of whose birth these triumphs are,
Sits here, like beauty's child, whom nature gat

For men to see, and seeing wonder at.

Tell them that we are ready; and my daughter,
whose birthday these festivities are celebrating,
is sitting here, like a child of beauty, whom
nature made
for men to see, and seeing be astonished by.

Exit a Lord

THAISA
It pleaseth you, my royal father, to express
My commendations great, whose merit's less.

You like to exaggerate my virtues, father,
I don't deserve it.

SIMONIDES
It's fit it should be so; for princes are
A model which heaven makes like to itself:
As jewels lose their glory if neglected,

So princes their renowns if not respected.

'Tis now your honour, daughter, to entertain
The labour of each knight in his device.

That's how it should be; for princes are
the models heaven makes of itself:
jewels will lose their brightness if they're not
polished,
and princes their reputations if they are not
respected.
It's now your privilege, daughter, to welcome
each knight according to the coat of arms on his
shield.

THAISA
Which, to preserve mine honour, I'll perform.

Which I will do, as befits my position.

Enter a Knight; he passes over, and his Squire presents his shield to the Princess

SIMONIDES
Who is the first that doth prefer himself?

Who is the first one who puts himself forward?

THAISA
A knight of Sparta, my renowned father;
And the device he bears upon his shield
Is a black Ethiope reaching at the sun
The word, 'Lux tua vita mihi.'

A knight of Sparta, my renowned father;
the picture he has on his shield
is of a black Ethiopian reaching out to the sun,
with the words, 'Your light is life to me.'

SIMONIDES
He loves you well that holds his life of you.

The one who rules over you loves you well.

The Second Knight passes over

Who is the second that presents himself?

Who is the second who presents himself?

THAISA
A prince of Macedon, my royal father;
And the device he bears upon his shield
Is an arm'd knight that's conquer'd by a lady;

The motto thus, in Spanish, 'Piu por dulzura que por
 fuerza.'

A prince of Macedonia, my royal father;
and the picture on his shield
is of an armed knight who is conquered by a lady;
the motto in Spanish is, 'More by gentleness than by force.'

The Third Knight passes over

SIMONIDES
And what's the third?

And who is the third?

THAISA
The third of Antioch;
And his device, a wreath of chivalry;
The word, 'Me pompae provexit apex.'

The third is from Antioch;
his symbol is a chivalric wreath;
the motto is, 'The desire for triumph drives me on.'

The Fourth Knight passes over

SIMONIDES
What is the fourth?

Who's the fourth?

THAISA
A burning torch that's turned upside down;
The word, 'Quod me alit, me extinguit.'

A burning torch that's upside down;
the motto, 'The one who feeds me puts me out.'

SIMONIDES
Which shows that beauty hath his power and will,

Which can as well inflame as it can kill.

Which shows that beauty has a power and desire,
which can light up just as well as it can kill.

The Fifth Knight passes over

THAISA
The fifth, an hand environed with clouds,
Holding out gold that's by the touchstone tried;

The motto thus, 'Sic spectanda fides.'

The fifth is a hand surrounded by clouds,
holding out gold that has been tested for genuineness;
the motto is, 'So you can test my faithfulness.'

The Sixth Knight, PERICLES, passes over

SIMONIDES

And what's
The sixth and last, the which the knight himself
With such a graceful courtesy deliver'd?

THAISA
He seems to be a stranger; but his present is
A wither'd branch, that's only green at top;
The motto, 'In hac spe vivo.'

SIMONIDES
A pretty moral;
From the dejected state wherein he is,
He hopes by you his fortunes yet may flourish.

First Lord
He had need mean better than his outward show

Can any way speak in his just commend;
For by his rusty outside he appears
To have practised more the whipstock than the lance.

Second Lord
He well may be a stranger, for he comes
To an honour'd triumph strangely furnished.

Third Lord
And on set purpose let his armour rust

Until this day, to scour it in the dust.

SIMONIDES
Opinion's but a fool, that makes us scan
The outward habit by the inward man.
But stay, the knights are coming: we will withdraw
Into the gallery.

Exeunt

Great shouts within and all cry 'The mean knight!'

And what is
the sixth and last, which the knight himself
handed over with such an elegant bow?

He seems to be a foreigner; his emblem is
a withered branch, that's only green at the top;
the motto is, 'I live for this hope.'

A nice motto;
from the lowly state he is in now,
he hopes to improve himself through you.

His intentions will have to be better than his
outward appearance
which doesn't exactly recommend him;
from his rusty armour he seems
more like a carter than a knight.

He may well be a foreigner, for he's very
strangely dressed for an important festival.

He seems to have deliberately let his armour
rust,
until today, when it will be rubbed clean in the
dust.

Opinion's just an idiocy, it makes us think
we can tell the inner man from his appearance.
But wait, here come the knights: we shall go
into the grandstand.

(Great shouts from within and all cry, "The poor
knight!)

SCENE III. The same. A hall of state: a banquet prepared.

Enter SIMONIDES, THAISA, Lords, Attendants, and Knights, from tilting

SIMONIDES
Knights,
To say you're welcome were superfluous.
To place upon the volume of your deeds,
As in a title-page, your worth in arms,

Were more than you expect, or more than's fit,

Since every worth in show commends itself.
Prepare for mirth, for mirth becomes a feast:

You are princes and my guests.

THAISA
But you, my knight and guest;
To whom this wreath of victory I give,
And crown you king of this day's happiness.

PERICLES
'Tis more by fortune, lady, than by merit.

SIMONIDES
Call it by what you will, the day is yours;
And here, I hope, is none that envies it.
In framing an artist, art hath thus decreed,
To make some good, but others to exceed;
And you are her labour'd scholar. Come, queen o'
the feast,--
For, daughter, so you are,--here take your place:
Marshal, the rest, as they deserve their grace.

KNIGHTS
We are honour'd much by good Simonides.

SIMONIDES
Your presence glads our days: honour we love;
For who hates honour hates the gods above.

Marshal
Sir, yonder is your place.

Knights,
it's not necessary to say that you're welcome.
To make a list of everything you've done,
as if writing a title page, your achievements with
arms,
is more than you would expect, or more than is
necessary,
since all your merits are obvious to see.
Get ready to enjoy yourselves, for feasts should
be enjoyed:
you are princes and my guests.

But you, my knight and guest;
I give you this victory wreath,
and crown you king of this happy day.

It was more by luck, lady, than through skill.

Call it what you want, you are the winner;
and I trust nobody begrudges you your victory.
When making an artist, art has ruled
that some will be good, but others exceptional;
you are her favourite pupil. Now, queen of
the feast—for that is what you are, daughter—
take your seat here:
Marshall, seat all the rest in order of
precedence.

We appreciate the honour good Simonides gives
us.

Your presence makes me happy: I love honour;
anyone who hates honour hates the gods above.

Sir, your place is there.

PERICLES
Some other is more fit.

Another would be more suitable.

First Knight
Contend not, sir; for we are gentlemen
That neither in our hearts nor outward eyes
Envy the great nor do the low despise.

*Do not argue, sir; we are gentlemen
who do not envy the great nor hate the low,
neither in our hearts or our behaviour.*

PERICLES
You are right courteous knights.

You are truly courteous knights.

SIMONIDES
Sit, sir, sit.

Sit, sit, sit.

PERICLES
By Jove, I wonder, that is king of thoughts,
These cates resist me, she but thought upon.

*By Jove, who is the king of thoughts, I'm amazed
that my thoughts of her quite put me off these
delicacies.*

THAISA
By Juno, that is queen of marriage,
All viands that I eat do seem unsavoury,
Wishing him my meat. Sure, he's a gallant gentleman.

*By Juno, who is the queen of marriage,
all the food I eat seems tasteless,
wishing to taste him. He certainly is a gallant
gentleman.*

SIMONIDES
He's but a country gentleman;
Has done no more than other knights have done;
Has broken a staff or so; so let it pass.

*He's just a country gentleman;
he has done no more than other knights;
he's broken a lance or two; forget it.*

THAISA
To me he seems like diamond to glass.

To me he's like a diamond compared to glass.

PERICLES
Yon king's to me like to my father's picture,
Which tells me in that glory once he was;
Had princes sit, like stars, about his throne,

And he the sun, for them to reverence;
None that beheld him, but, like lesser lights,

Did vail their crowns to his supremacy:

Where now his son's like a glow-worm in the night,
The which hath fire in darkness, none in light:

*The King reminds me of my father's picture,
which showed me how glorious he once was;
he had princes sitting, like stars, around his
throne,
with him as the sun, for them to worship;
nobody who saw him could help but, like smaller
stars,
to have the light of their crown eclipsed by his
supremacy:
now his son is like a glowworm in the night,
which only shines in the darkness, not in the
light:*

Whereby I see that Time's the king of men,
He's both their parent, and he is their grave,
And gives them what he will, not what they crave.

through this I can see that time rules over men,
he is their parent and their gravedigger,
and he gives them what he decides, not what
they want.

SIMONIDES
What, are you merry, knights?

Are you enjoying yourselves, knights?

Knights
Who can be other in this royal presence?

How could we not be in your royal presence?

SIMONIDES
Here, with a cup that's stored unto the brim,--
As you do love, fill to your mistress' lips,--
We drink this health to you.

Here, with a cup that is full to the brim—
as you love her, lift it to your mistress' lips—
we drink your health.

KNIGHTS
We thank your grace.

We thank your grace.

SIMONIDES
Yet pause awhile:
Yon knight doth sit too melancholy,
As if the entertainment in our court
Had not a show might countervail his worth.
Note it not you, Thaisa?

But just a minute:
that knight there looks too miserable,
as if the entertainment at our court
wasn't good enough for him.
Do you see it, Thaisa?

THAIS
What is it
To me, my father?

Why should I care,
father?

SIMONIDES
O, attend, my daughter:
Princes in this should live like gods above,
Who freely give to every one that comes
To honour them:
And princes not doin g so are like to gnats,
Which make a sound, but kill'd are wonder'd at.

Therefore to make his entertainment more sweet,
Here, say we drink this standing-bowl of wine to him.

Pay attention, my daughter:
in matters like this princes should live like gods,
who give freely to everyone who comes
to honour them:
Princes who do not do so are like gnats,
which make a sound which can't be believed
when they killed.
So, to cheer him up,
tell him we drink a toast to him.

THAISA
Alas, my father, it befits not me
Unto a stranger knight to be so bold:
He may my proffer take for an offence,
Since men take women's gifts for impudence.

Alas, my father, it's not my place
to be so forward with an unknown knight:
he might take offence at my offer,
since men look at women's gifts as impertinence.

SIMONIDES

How!
Do as I bid you, or you'll move me else.

What!
Do as you're told, or you'll make me angry.

THAISA
[Aside] Now, by the gods, he could not please me better.

By the gods, nothing could make me happier.

SIMONIDES
And furthermore tell him, we desire to know of him,
Of whence he is, his name and parentage.

And also tell him, I want to know about him,
where he's come from, his name and his
ancestry.

THAISA
The king my father, sir, has drunk to you.

My father the king, sir, has drunk your health.

PERICLES
I thank him.

I thank him.

THAISA
Wishing it so much blood unto your life.

And he wishes you a long life.

PERICLES
I thank both him and you, and pledge him freely.

I thank both him and you, and gladly drink to
you.

THAISA
And further he desires to know of you,
Of whence you are, your name and parentage.

And he wants to know more about you,
where you've come from, your name and
ancestry.

PERICLES
A gentleman of Tyre; my name, Pericles;
My education been in arts and arms;
Who, looking for adventures in the world,
Was by the rough seas reft of ships and men,

And after shipwreck driven upon this shore.

I am a gentleman of Tyre; my name is Pericles;
I have been tutored in arts and arms;
seeking adventure in the world,
I had my ships and men stolen from me by rough
seas,
and after I was shipwrecked I was washed up on
this shore

THAISA
He thanks your grace; names himself Pericles,

A gentleman of Tyre,
Who only by misfortune of the seas
Bereft of ships and men, cast on this shore.

He thanks your grace; he says his name is
Pericles,
a gentleman of Tyre,
who through a mishap on the sea
lost his ships and men, and was washed up on
this shore.

SIMONIDES

Now, by the gods, I pity his misfortune,
And will awake him from his melancholy.
Come, gentlemen, we sit too long on trifles,

And waste the time, which looks for other revels.

Even in your armours, as you are address'd,
Will very well become a soldier's dance.
I will not have excuse, with saying this
Loud music is too harsh for ladies' heads,
Since they love men in arms as well as beds.

The Knights dance
So, this was well ask'd,'twas so well perform'd.
Come, sir;
Here is a lady that wants breathing too:
And I have heard, you knights of Tyre
Are excellent in making ladies trip;
And that their measures are as excellent.

PERICLES
In those that practise them they are, my lord.

SIMONIDES
O, that's as much as you would be denied
Of your fair courtesy.

The Knights and Ladies dance
Unclasp, unclasp:
Thanks, gentlemen, to all; all have done well.

To PERICLES
But you the best. Pages and lights, to conduct

These knights unto their several lodgings!

To PERICLES
Yours, sir,
We have given order to be next our own.

PERICLES
I am at your grace's pleasure.

SIMONIDES
Princes, it is too late to talk of love;
And that's the mark I know you level at:

*Now, by the gods, I pity his misfortune,
and I will bring him out of his sadness.
Come on, gentlemen, we've been sitting too long
over food,
and wasting time which could be spent on other
entertainment.
As you are all dressed in your armour
that's very suitable for a soldier's dance.
I'll have no excuses with people saying
such things are too rough for the ladies,
because they love men in armour as well as in
their beds.*

*This performance honoured my request.
Come, sir, there's a lady here who needs
exercise;
and I have heard that the knights of Tyre
are excellent dancers with the ladies,
in a light skipping dance or a formal one.*

Those who practice dancing are, my lord.

Oh, that's enough of your polite modesty.

*Let them go, let them go:
thank you, gentlemen, all of you, you all danced
well–*

*But you were the best. Servants and torches
here,
to guide these knights to their bedrooms!*

*I have ordered, sir,
that you should be lodged next door to me.*

Whatever your grace chooses.

*Princes, it is too late to talk about love:
and I know that's what you're all thinking about:*

Therefore each one betake him to his rest;
To-morrow all for speeding do their best.

Exeunt

so each of you go and get your rest;
tomorrow you can all do your best to win.

SCENE IV. Tyre. A room in the Governor's house.

Enter HELICANUS and ESCANES

HELICANUS
No, Escanes, know this of me,
Antiochus from incest lived not free:

For which, the most high gods not minding longer
To withhold the vengeance that they had in store,

Due to this heinous capital offence,
Even in the height and pride of all his glory,
When he was seated in a chariot
Of an inestimable value, and his daughter with him,
A fire from heaven came and shrivell'd up
Their bodies, even to loathing; for they so stunk,

That all those eyes adored them ere their fall

Scorn now their hand should give them burial.

ESCANES
'Twas very strange.

HELICANUS
And yet but justice; for though
This king were great, his greatness was no guard

To bar heaven's shaft, but sin had his reward.

ESCANES
'Tis very true.

Enter two or three Lords

First Lord
See, not a man in private conference
Or council has respect with him but he.

Second Lord
It shall no longer grieve without reproof.

Third Lord
And cursed be he that will not second it.

No, Escanes, I can tell you this,
Antiochus did not escape unpunished for his
incest:
the great gods decided to no longer
hold back the punishment they had in store for
him,
due to his appalling offence;
even as he sat in his luxurious chariot
at the height of all his pride and glory,
with his daughter by his side,
fire struck from heaven and shrivelled up
their bodies until they were a foul sight to see:
they stank so badly
that all those people who worshipped them
before
refuse to even touch them to give them a burial.

It was very strange.

But it was only justice; although
this king was great, his greatness was no
protection
against the powers of heaven, so he got what he
deserved.

That's very true.

You see, he respects no man's opinion, in
private conference or in council, but his own.

It shall no longer carry on uncritcised.

And damnation to anyone who will not agree.

46

First Lord
Follow me, then. Lord Helicane, a word.

Follow me, then. Lord Helicanus, a word with you.

HELICANUS
With me? and welcome: happy day, my lords.

With me? You're welcome to it: good day to you, my lords.

First Lord
Know that our griefs are risen to the top,

And now at length they overflow their banks.

I tell you that our flood of grievances has swollen
to the point where they will now burst their banks.

HELICANUS
Your griefs! for what? wrong not your prince you love.

Your grievances! For what? Do not wrong the prince you love.

First Lord
Wrong not yourself, then, noble Helicane;
But if the prince do live, let us salute him,
Or know what ground's made happy by his breath.
If in the world he live, we'll seek him out;
If in his grave he rest, we'll find him there;
And be resolved he lives to govern us,
Or dead, give's cause to mourn his funeral,
And leave us to our free election.

Do not wrong yourself, then, noble Helicanus;
but if the Prince is alive, let us salute him,
or at least know where he is.
If he is alive somewhere, we'll look for him;
if he is in his grave, will find him there;
if he is alive he should be governing us,
if he is dead, let us mourn him
and proceed to choose a new leader.

Second Lord
Whose death indeed's the strongest in our censure:
And knowing this kingdom is without a head,--
Like goodly buildings left without a roof
Soon fall to ruin,--your noble self,
That best know how to rule and how to reign,

We thus submit unto,--our sovereign.

It seems most likely that he is dead:
and as this kingdom is now leaderless—
and like strong buildings left without a roof
will soon be ruined—we ask your noble self,
who knows best of all how to rule and how to reign,
to allow us to accept you as our king.

All
Live, noble Helicane!

Long live noble Helicanus!

HELICANUS
For honour's cause, forbear your suffrages:

If that you love Prince Pericles, forbear.
Take I your wish, I leap into the seas,

Where's hourly trouble for a minute's ease.

For the sake of honour, do not make such a choice:
if you still love Prince Pericles, hold off.
If I allowed your wish I would be jumping into seas
where there's lifelong trouble for the sake of

A twelvemonth longer, let me entreat you to
Forbear the absence of your king:
If in which time expired, he not return,
I shall with aged patience bear your yoke.

But if I cannot win you to this love,
Go search like nobles, like noble subjects,
And in your search spend your adventurous worth;
Whom if you find, and win unto return,
You shall like diamonds sit about his crown.

First Lord
To wisdom he's a fool that will not yield;
And since Lord Helicane enjoineth us,
We with our travels will endeavour us.

HELICANUS
Then you love us, we you, and we'll clasp hands:

When peers thus knit, a kingdom ever stands.

Exeunt

minute's pleasure.
Let me beg you to tolerate
the absence of your king for one more year:
if he has not returned when that time is up,
I will take on your request with my aged
patience.
But if I cannot persuade you to do this,
go and search like noblemen, like noble subjects,
using all your courage in the search;
if you find him, and persuade him to return,
you will be like diamonds in his crown.

Only a fool will not follow wise advice;
and since Lord Helicanus asks us,
we will undertake this journey.

Then you love me, I you, and we'll shake hands
on it:
when lords stand together like this, the kingdom
cannot fall.

SCENE V. Pentapolis. A room in the palace.

Enter SIMONIDES, reading a letter, at one door: the Knights meet him

First Knight
Good morrow to the good Simonides.

Good day to good Simonides.

SIMONIDES
Knights, from my daughter this I let you know,
That for this twelvemonth she'll not undertake
A married life.
Her reason to herself is only known,
Which yet from her by no means can I get.

Knights, I must tell you this from my daughter,
that she refuses to get married for the next
year.
Only she knows the reason for this,
and she will not tell me it.

Second Knight
May we not get access to her, my lord?

Can we not speak to her, my lord?

SIMONIDES
'Faith, by no means; she has so strictly tied
Her to her chamber, that 'tis impossible.
One twelve moons more she'll wear Diana's livery;
This by the eye of Cynthia hath she vow'd
And on her virgin honour will not break it.

Definitely not; she has locked herself so securely
in her rooms that it is impossible.
She will remain a virgin for another year;
she has sworn this by the goddess Diana
and she will not break her maidenly vow.

Third Knight
Loath to bid farewell, we take our leaves.

Though we hate to say farewell, we shall leave.

Exeunt Knights

SIMONIDES
So,
They are well dispatch'd; now to my daughter's letter:

She tells me here, she'd wed the stranger knight,

Or never more to view nor day nor light.
'Tis well, mistress; your choice agrees with mine;
I like that well: nay, how absolute she's in't,
Not minding whether I dislike or no!
Well, I do commend her choice;
And will no longer have it be delay'd.
Soft! here he comes: I must dissemble it.

So,
they are on their way; now for my daughter's
letter:
she tells me here that she will marry the foreign
knight,
or never see daylight again.
That's fine, mistress; that's my choice too;
that pleases me: still, how determined she is,
not caring whether I approve or not!
Well, I approve the choice;
and want the matter progressed without delay.
Hush! Here he comes: I must keep it secret.

Enter PERICLES

PERICLES

All fortune to the good Simonides!

SIMONIDES
To you as much, sir! I am beholding to you
For your sweet music this last night: I do

Protest my ears were never better fed
With such delightful pleasing harmony.

PERICLES
It is your grace's pleasure to commend;
Not my desert.

SIMONIDES
Sir, you are music's master.

PERICLES
The worst of all her scholars, my good lord.

SIMONIDES
Let me ask you one thing:
What do you think of my daughter, sir?

PERICLES
A most virtuous princess.

SIMONIDES
And she is fair too, is she not?

PERICLES
As a fair day in summer, wondrous fair.

SIMONIDES
Sir, my daughter thinks very well of you;
Ay, so well, that you must be her master,
And she will be your scholar: therefore look to it.

PERICLES
I am unworthy for her schoolmaster.

SIMONIDES
She thinks not so; peruse this writing else.

PERICLES
[Aside] What's here?
A letter, that she loves the knight of Tyre!
'Tis the king's subtlety to have my life.
O, seek not to entrap me, gracious lord,

All blessings to the good Simonides!

*And the same to you, sir! I am grateful to you
for the sweet music you gave us last night: I
must
say that my ears never heard
such delightful pleasant harmonies.*

*It is kind of your grace to say so,
but I don't deserve it.*

Sir, you are a master of music.

I'm the worst of all her students, my good lord.

*Let me ask you one thing:
what do you think my daughter, sir?*

A very virtuous princess.

And she is beautiful too, isn't she?

As a lovely summer's day, amazingly beautiful.

*Sir, my daughter thinks a lot of you;
so much so she wants you as a master,
and she will be your student: so proceed.*

I am not worthy to be her schoolmaster.

She doesn't think so; have a look at this letter.

*What's this?
A letter, saying she loves the Knight of Tyre!
This is a trap to keep me here for life.
Oh, do not try to trap me, gracious lord,*

A stranger and distressed gentleman,
That never aim'd so high to love your daughter,

But bent all offices to honour her.

SIMONIDES
Thou hast bewitch'd my daughter, and thou art
A villain.

PERICLES
By the gods, I have not:
Never did thought of mine levy offence;
Nor never did my actions yet commence
A deed might gain her love or your displeasure.

SIMONIDES
Traitor, thou liest.

PERICLES
Traitor!

SIMONIDES
Ay, traitor.

PERICLES
Even in his throat--unless it be the king--
That calls me traitor, I return the lie.

SIMONIDES
[Aside] Now, by the gods, I do applaud his courage.

PERICLES
My actions are as noble as my thoughts,
That never relish'd of a base descent.
I came unto your court for honour's cause,
And not to be a rebel to her state;
And he that otherwise accounts of me,
This sword shall prove he's honour's enemy.

SIMONIDES
No?
Here comes my daughter, she can witness it.

Enter THAISA

PERICLES
Then, as you are as virtuous as fair,

a foreigner and distressed gentleman,
who never aimed so high as to love your
daughter,
but tried to honour her in every way.

You have bewitched my daughter, and you are
a villain.

I swear by the gods, I have not:
I have done nothing wrong in my thoughts
nor in my actions, I've done no deed
which might gain her love or your displeasure.

Traitor, you lie.

Traitor!

Yes, traitor.

If anyone except for the king calls me
a traitor, I'll throw it back in his face.

Now, by the gods, I admire his courage.

My actions are as pure as my thoughts,
that never had a trace of anything vulgar.
I came to your court for the sake of honour,
not to undermine its majesty;
if anyone says differently about me,
this sword will prove him a liar.

Really?
Here comes my daughter, she can vouch for it.

Then, as you are as good as you're beautiful,

Resolve your angry father, if my tongue
Did ere solicit, or my hand subscribe
To any syllable that made love to you.

THAISA
Why, sir, say if you had,
Who takes offence at that would make me glad?

SIMONIDES
Yea, mistress, are you so peremptory?

Aside
I am glad on't with all my heart.--
I'll tame you; I'll bring you in subjection.
Will you, not having my consent,
Bestow your love and your affections
Upon a stranger?

Aside
who, for aught I know,
May be, nor can I think the contrary,
As great in blood as I myself.--
Therefore hear you, mistress; either frame
Your will to mine,--and you, sir, hear you,
Either be ruled by me, or I will make you--
Man and wife:
Nay, come, your hands and lips must seal it too:

And being join'd, I'll thus your hopes destroy;

And for a further grief,--God give you joy!--

What, are you both pleased?

THAISA
Yes, if you love me, sir.

PERICLES
Even as my life, or blood that fosters it.

SIMONIDES
What, are you both agreed?

BOTH
Yes, if it please your majesty.

SIMONIDES

tell your angry father if my tongue
ever uttered, or my hand ever wrote,
any syllable saying I loved you.

Why, sir, in the event that you had,
who would take offence at something that would
make me glad?

So, mistress, you've decided on this?

[Aside] I'm glad of this with all my heart–
I'll tame you, I'll make you obey.

Will you give your love and affection
to a stranger, without my consent? [Aside] Who,

for all I know, might be (and I think is)

as highborn as I am myself–
now listen to me, mistress: either do
as I say; and you, sir, listen:
if you don't do as I say I shall make you–
man and wife.
Come on now, your hands and lips must seal the
bargain;
being joined like this, I'll further destroy your
hopes,
and give you more grief, by saying, may God
give you joy!
So, are you both happy with this?

Yes, if you love me, sir.

As much as my life, or the blood that sustains it.

So, you are both agreed?

Yes, if it pleases your Majesty.

It pleaseth me so well, that I will see you wed;

And then with what haste you can get you to bed.

It makes me so pleased, that I want to see you married;

and then you can go to bed as quickly as you like.

Exeunt

Act 3

SCENE I.

Enter GOWER

GOWER

Now sleep y-slaked hath the rout;	Now sleep has calmed the revelry;
No din but snores the house about,	the only sound in the house is snores,
Made louder by the o'er-fed breast	made louder by the overfeeding
Of this most pompous marriage-feast.	of this magnificent wedding feast.
The cat, with eyne of burning coal,	The cat, with eyes like burning coals,
Now crouches fore the mouse's hole;	now sleeps in front of the mouse's hole;
And crickets sing at the oven's mouth,	and crickets by the oven door
E'er the blither for their drouth.	sing more sweetly in the heat.
Hymen hath brought the bride to bed.	The goddess Hymen has brought the bride to bed,
Where, by the loss of maidenhead,	and in her loss of virginity
A babe is moulded. Be attent,	a baby is conceived. Pay attention,
And time that is so briefly spent	and eke out this brief display
With your fine fancies quaintly eche:	with your great imaginations;
What's dumb in show I'll plain with speech.	I shall explain this dumb show with speech.

DUMB SHOW.

Enter, PERICLES and SIMONIDES at one door, with Attendants; a Messenger meets them, kneels, and gives PERICLES a letter: PERICLES shows it SIMONIDES; the Lords kneel to him. Then enter THAISA with child, with LYCHORIDA a nurse. The KING shows her the letter; she rejoices: she and PERICLES takes leave of her father, and depart with LYCHORIDA and their Attendants. Then exeunt SIMONIDES and the rest	Enter, PERICLES and SIMONIDES at one door, with Attendants; a Messenger meets them, kneels, and gives PERICLES a letter: PERICLES shows it SIMONIDES; the Lords kneel to him. Then enter THAISA with child, with LYCHORIDA a nurse. The KING shows her the letter; she rejoices: she and PERICLES takes leave of her father, and depart with LYCHORIDA and their Attendants. Then exeunt SIMONIDES and the rest.

By many a dern and painful perch	With many dark and dangerous journeys
Of Pericles the careful search,	Pericles is sought
By the four opposing coigns	in all four corners
Which the world together joins,	of the world,
Is made with all due diligence	with all the efforts
That horse and sail and high expense	that horses and ships and great expense
Can stead the quest. At last from Tyre,	can muster. At last from the unfamiliar
Fame answering the most strange inquire,	land of Tyre comes an enquiry, prompted
To the court of King Simonides	by rumours, to the court of King Simonides,
Are letters brought, the tenor these:	and letters arrive, telling this story:
Antiochus and his daughter dead;	that Antiochus and his daughter are dead,
The men of Tyrus on the head	and that the people of Tyre want
Of Helicanus would set on	to crown Helicanus as their king,
The crown of Tyre, but he will none:	but he will not accept:

The mutiny he there hastes t' oppress;
Says to 'em, if King Pericles
Come not home in twice six moons,
He, obedient to their dooms,
Will take the crown. The sum of this,
Brought hither to Pentapolis,
Y-ravished the regions round,
And every one with claps can sound,
'Our heir-apparent is a king!
Who dream'd, who thought of such a thing?'
Brief, he must hence depart to Tyre:
His queen with child makes her desire--
Which who shall cross?--along to go:
Omit we all their dole and woe:

Lychorida, her nurse, she takes,
And so to sea. Their vessel shakes
On Neptune's billow; half the flood
Hath their keel cut: but fortune's mood
Varies again; the grisly north
Disgorges such a tempest forth,
That, as a duck for life that dives,
So up and down the poor ship drives:
The lady shrieks, and well-a-near
Does fall in travail with her fear:
And what ensues in this fell storm
Shall for itself itself perform.
I nill relate, action may
Conveniently the rest convey;
Which might not what by me is told.
In your imagination hold
This stage the ship, upon whose deck
The sea-tost Pericles appears to speak.

he quickly averts any rebellion
by saying to them that if King Pericles
is not home within a year
he will accede to their wishes
and take the crown. This information,
brought to Pentapolis,
astonished the whole country
and everyone began to applaud and say,
"Our heir apparent is a king!
Whoever dreamed such a thing possible?"
To sum up, he must leave for Tyre.
His pregnant queen requests–
and who can deny her?–to accompany him.
We shall omit all their grief and sorrow at
leaving.
Lychordia, her nurse, goes with them,
and they set out on the sea. Their ship is shaken
upon the waves; they have crossed
half the sea; but then the mood of fate
changes again; the stormy North
unleashes such a tempest
that the ship tosses up and down
like a duck diving for its life.
The lady shrieks and, alas,
the fear starts her labour;
what follows in this dreadful storm
shall be shown to you now.
I won't say more, the action will
be better to show you the rest;
I have just covered what it might have missed.
In your imagination think that
this stage is the ship, on the deck of which
the storm-tossed Pericles appears to speak.

Exit

SCENE I:

Enter PERICLES, on shipboard

PERICLES
Thou god of this great vast, rebuke these surges,
Which wash both heaven and hell; and thou, that hast
Upon the winds command, bind them in brass,
Having call'd them from the deep! O, still
Thy deafening, dreadful thunders; gently quench
Thy nimble, sulphurous flashes! O, how, Lychorida,
How does my queen? Thou stormest venomously;

O God of this great ocean, calm these waves,
which wash over both heaven and hell; and as
you command all winds, lock them up again,
having summoned them from the deep! Oh stop
your deafening dreadful thunder; extinguish
the flashes of lightning! O Lychordia,
how is my queen? The storm is fierce;

Wilt thou spit all thyself? The seaman's whistle

Is as a whisper in the ears of death,
Unheard. Lychorida!--Lucina, O
Divinest patroness, and midwife gentle
To those that cry by night, convey thy deity

Aboard our dancing boat; make swift the pangs
Of my queen's travails!

Enter LYCHORIDA, with an Infant
Now, Lychorida!

LYCHORIDA
Here is a thing too young for such a place,
Who, if it had conceit, would die, as I
Am like to do: take in your arms this piece
Of your dead queen.

PERICLES
How, how, Lychorida!

LYCHORIDA
Patience, good sir; do not assist the storm.
Here's all that is left living of your queen,
A little daughter: for the sake of it,
Be manly, and take comfort.

PERICLES
O you gods!
Why do you make us love your goodly gifts,
And snatch them straight away? We here below

Recall not what we give, and therein may
Use honour with you.

LYCHORIDA
Patience, good sir,
Even for this charge.

PERICLES
Now, mild may be thy life!
For a more blustrous birth had never babe:
Quiet and gentle thy conditions! for
Thou art the rudeliest welcome to this world
That ever was prince's child. Happy what follows!

Thou hast as chiding a nativity

will you tear yourself to pieces? The sailor's whistle
is like a whisper in the ears of the dead,
it goes unheard. Lychordia! Lucina, you heavenly patroness, and gentle midwife
to those who cry in the night, bring your godliness
onto our tossing boat; ease the pains
of my queen's labour! Now, Lychordia!

Here is a thing too young for such a place,
if it had understanding it would die, as I
am likely to do: take in your arms this remnant
of your dead queen.

What, what, Lychordia!

Be calm, good sir; do not add to the storm.
Here is all that is still alive of your queen,
a little daughter: for its sake,
be a man, and take this consolation.

Oh you gods!
Why do you make us love your wonderful gifts,
and then snatch them straight away? We here below
do not take back what we give, and then
use it against you.

Be calm, good sir,
if only for the sake of the baby.

Now, may your life be quiet!
No baby ever had a more stormy birth:
may your life be calm and gentle! For
you had the roughest welcome into the world
a prince's child ever had. May what follows be happy!
You have had as noisy a birth

As fire, air, water, earth, and heaven can make,
To herald thee from the womb: even at the first

Thy loss is more than can thy portage quit,
With all thou canst find here. Now, the good gods

Throw their best eyes upon't!

as fire, air, water, earth and heaven could make,
to announce you from the womb: right from the start
you have suffered a loss which nothing you find
on earth will make up for. Now, may the good gods
do their best for you!

Enter two Sailors

First Sailor
What courage, sir? God save you!

What hope is there, sir? May God save you!

PERICLES
Courage enough: I do not fear the flaw;
It hath done to me the worst. Yet, for the love

Of this poor infant, this fresh-new sea-farer,
I would it would be quiet.

There is hope enough: I do not fear the gales;
they have done the worst to me they can. But, out of love
for this poor child, this brand-new sailor,
I wish it would be calm.

First Sailor
Slack the bolins there! Thou wilt not, wilt thou?
Blow, and split thyself.

Slacken the bow lines there! Oh so you won't?
Then blow yourself out.

Second Sailor
But sea-room, an the brine and cloudy billow kiss

the moon, I care not.

As long as we have the open sea the waves and spray can kiss
the moon, I don't care.

First Sailor
Sir, your queen must overboard: the sea works high,

the wind is loud, and will not lie till the ship be

cleared of the dead.

Sir, your queen must go overboard: the sea's running high,
the wind is fierce, and it will not calm until the ship is
emptied of the dead.

PERICLES
That's your superstition.

That's your superstition.

First Sailor
Pardon us, sir; with us at sea it hath been still
observed: and we are strong in custom. Therefore

briefly yield her; for she must overboard straight.

Excuse us, sir; with those of us who sail it is still
believed, and we follow our traditions. Therefore
you must give her up at once; she must go straight overboard.

PERICLES
As you think meet. Most wretched queen!

Whatever you think best. Most wretched queen!

LYCHORIDA
Here she lies, sir.

She's lying here, sir.

PERICLES
A terrible childbed hast thou had, my dear;
No light, no fire: the unfriendly elements
Forgot thee utterly: nor have I time

A terrible maternity bed you had, my dear;
no light, no fire: the harsh elements
completely forgot about you: and I don't have
the time

To give thee hallow'd to thy grave, but straight
Must cast thee, scarcely coffin'd, in the ooze;

to hold a proper funeral, but must throw you
straight over the side, without a proper coffin,
into the sea;

Where, for a monument upon thy bones,
And e'er-remaining lamps, the belching whale
And humming water must o'erwhelm thy corpse,
Lying with simple shells. O Lychorida,
Bid Nestor bring me spices, ink and paper,
My casket and my jewels; and bid Nicander
Bring me the satin coffer: lay the babe
Upon the pillow: hie thee, whiles I say
A priestly farewell to her: suddenly, woman.

the marker over your grave will have to be
the eternal stars, the belching whale,
and the turbulent water must cover your corpse,
lying with simple shells. Oh Lychordia,
Tell Nestor to bring the spices, ink and paper,
my valuables box and my jewels; tell Nicander
to bring the satin chest; put the baby
on the pillow; do that, while I say
the burial service over her: quickly, woman.

Exit LYCHORIDA

Second Sailor
Sir, we have a chest beneath the hatches, caulked
and bitumed ready.

Sir, we have a chest beneath the hatches, all
ready and waterproofed.

PERICLES
I thank thee. Mariner, say what coast is this?

Thank you. Sailor, tell me what coast this is.

Second Sailor
We are near Tarsus.

We are near Tarsus.

PERICLES
Thither, gentle mariner,
Alter thy course for Tyre. When canst thou reach it?

Change your course from Tyre, good sailor,
and head for there. When can you reach it?

Second Sailor
By break of day, if the wind cease.

By morning, if the wind drops.

PERICLES
O, make for Tarsus!
There will I visit Cleon, for the babe
Cannot hold out to Tyrus: there I'll leave it
At careful nursing. Go thy ways, good mariner:

Oh, head for Tarsus!
I will visit Cleon there, because the baby
will not survive until Tyre: I'll leave it there,
well looked after. Go about your business, good
sailor:

I'll bring the body presently.

I'll bring the body along shortly.

58

Exeunt

SCENE II. Ephesus. A room in CERIMON's house.

Enter CERIMON, with a Servant, and some Persons who have been shipwrecked

CERIMON
Philemon, ho!

Philemon, come here!

Enter PHILEMON

PHILEMON
Doth my lord call?

Did my Lord call?

CERIMON
Get fire and meat for these poor men:
'T has been a turbulent and stormy night.

Get a fire and meat for these poor men:
it has been a windy and stormy night.

Servant
I have been in many; but such a night as this,
Till now, I ne'er endured.

I have been in many; but until now I never saw
a night such as this.

CERIMON
Your master will be dead ere you return;
There's nothing can be minister'd to nature
That can recover him.

Your master will be dead before you return;
there's nothing that can be given to him
which can save him.

To PHILEMON

Give this to the 'pothecary,
And tell me how it works.

Give this to the chemist,
and tell me how it goes.

Exeunt all but CERIMON

Enter two Gentlemen

First Gentleman
Good morrow.

Good day.

Second Gentleman
Good morrow to your lordship.

Good day to your lordship.

CERIMON
Gentlemen,
Why do you stir so early?

Gentlemen,
why are you up so early?

First Gentleman
Sir,
Our lodgings, standing bleak upon the sea,

Sir,
our lodgings, standing right next to the sea,

60

Shook as the earth did quake;
The very principals did seem to rend,
And all-to topple: pure surprise and fear
Made me to quit the house.

Second Gentleman
That is the cause we trouble you so early;
'Tis not our husbandry.

CERIMON
O, you say well.

First Gentleman
But I much marvel that your lordship, having
Rich tire about you, should at these early hours

Shake off the golden slumber of repose.
'Tis most strange,
Nature should be so conversant with pain,
Being thereto not compell'd.

CERIMON
I hold it ever,
Virtue and cunning were endowments greater
Than nobleness and riches: careless heirs
May the two latter darken and expend;
But immortality attends the former,
Making a man a god. 'Tis known, I ever
Have studied physic, through which secret art,
By turning o'er authorities, I have,
Together with my practise, made familiar
To me and to my aid the blest infusions
That dwell in vegetives, in metals, stones;
And I can speak of the disturbances
That nature works, and of her cures; which doth give me
A more content in course of true delight
Than to be thirsty after tottering honour,
Or tie my treasure up in silken bags,
To please the fool and death.

Second Gentleman
Your honour has through Ephesus pour'd forth
Your charity, and hundreds call themselves

Your creatures, who by you have been restored:
And not your knowledge, your personal pain, but even
Your purse, still open, hath built Lord Cerimon

shook as the earth shook;
the very foundations seemed to break,
and be about to fall: sheer surprise and fear
made me leave the house.

This is why we are here so early;
it's not an eagerness to work.

Oh, you speak well.

But I'm astonished that your lordship, with
such strong buildings around you, should so early
Shake off the golden peace of sleep.
It's very strange,
that you should want to suffer this discomfort,
when you are not forced to.

I have always said
that virtue and cunning are better things to have
than nobility and wealth: careless heirs
can stain and spend the latter;
the former lasts forever,
making man a God. You know I have always
studied medicine, and through that secret art,
by reading the works of masters, I have,
combined with my experiments, made myself
and my assistant familiar with the substances
which dwell in plants, in metals and stones;
I can describe the disturbances that
nature causes, and how to cure them; this gives me
more genuine happiness
than to always be chasing worthless honours,
or storing up my treasure in silk bags,
to please the fool and death.

Your honour has spread your charity throughout
Ephesus, and hundreds who have been saved by you
call themselves your servants:
and your knowledge, your great efforts, and also
your generosity with money, have given the Lord

61

Such strong renown as time shall ne'er decay.

Cerimon
such great fame that he will never be forgotten.

Enter two or three Servants with a chest

First Servant
So; lift there.

That's it, lift your end.

CERIMON
What is that?

What's that?

First Servant
Sir, even now
Did the sea toss upon our shore this chest:
'Tis of some wreck.

Sir, just now
the sea washed this chest up on our shore:
it's from some wreck.

CERIMON
Set 't down, let's look upon't.

Put it down, let's have a look at it.

Second Gentleman
'Tis like a coffin, sir.

It's like a coffin, sir.

CERIMON
Whate'er it be,
'Tis wondrous heavy. Wrench it open straight:
If the sea's stomach be o'ercharged with gold,
'Tis a good constraint of fortune it belches upon us.

Whatever it is,
it's amazingly heavy. Tear it open at once:
if the sea has too much gold in its stomach,
it's a bit of luck that it's belched some up for us.

Second Gentleman
'Tis so, my lord.

That's right, my lord.

CERIMON
How close 'tis caulk'd and bitumed!
Did the sea cast it up?

How tightly it's waterproofed!
Did the sea throw it up?

First Servant
I never saw so huge a billow, sir,
As toss'd it upon shore.

I never saw such a great wave, sir,
as the one which threw it onto the shore.

CERIMON
Wrench it open;
Soft! it smells most sweetly in my sense.

Tear it open;
well! It smells very sweet to me.

Second Gentleman
A delicate odour.

A delicate odour.

CERIMON

As ever hit my nostril. So, up with it.
O you most potent gods! what's here? a corse!

First Gentleman
Most strange!

CERIMON
Shrouded in cloth of state; balm'd and entreasured

With full bags of spices! A passport too!
Apollo, perfect me in the characters!

Reads from a scroll
'Here I give to understand,
If e'er this coffin drive a-land,
I, King Pericles, have lost
This queen, worth all our mundane cost.
Who finds her, give her burying;
She was the daughter of a king:
Besides this treasure for a fee,
The gods requite his charity!'
If thou livest, Pericles, thou hast a heart
That even cracks for woe! This chanced tonight.

Second Gentleman
Most likely, sir.

CERIMON
Nay, certainly to-night;
For look how fresh she looks! They were too rough
That threw her in the sea. Make a fire within:

Fetch hither all my boxes in my closet.

Exit a Servant
Death may usurp on nature many hours,
And yet the fire of life kindle again
The o'erpress'd spirits. I heard of an Egyptian
That had nine hours lien dead,
Who was by good appliance recovered.

Re-enter a Servant, with boxes, napkins, and fire
Well said, well said; the fire and cloths.
The rough and woeful music that we have,
Cause it to sound, beseech you.
The viol once more: how thou stirr'st, thou block!

As sweet as I ever smelt. So, off with the lid.
Oh you powerful gods! What's this? A corpse!

Very strange!

Wrapped in royal robes; embalmed and packed round
with full bags of spices! A passport too!
Apollo, help me read what it says!

'I would like you to understand,
if this coffin ever reaches land,
I, King Pericles, have lost
this priceless queen.
If you find her then bury her;
she was the daughter of a king.
Take this treasure as your fee,
and may the gods bless you for your charity!'

If you are alive, Pericles, your heart
must be broken with sorrow! This happened last
night.

Very probably, sir.

Yes, it was certainly last night;
look how fresh she looks! They were too hasty
when they threw her into the sea. Light a fire
indoors;
bring me all the boxes from my cupboard.

Death can overcome a person for many hours,
and yet the sufferer can still
be brought back to life. I heard of an Egyptian
who lay dead for nine hours,
who was brought back to life with good
treatment.

Well done, well done; the fire and cloths.
I beg you, play what quiet
and sad music we have.
The violin again; you thickheaded slowcoach!

The music there!--I pray you, give her air.
Gentlemen.
This queen will live: nature awakes; a warmth
Breathes out of her: she hath not been entranced
Above five hours: see how she gins to blow

Into life's flower again!

First Gentleman
The heavens,
Through you, increase our wonder and set up
Your fame forever.

CERIMON
She is alive; behold,
Her eyelids, cases to those heavenly jewels
Which Pericles hath lost,
Begin to part their fringes of bright gold;
The diamonds of a most praised water
Do appear, to make the world twice rich. Live,
And make us weep to hear your fate, fair creature,

Rare as you seem to be.

She moves

THAISA
O dear Diana,
Where am I? Where's my lord? What world is this?

Second Gentleman
Is not this strange?

First Gentleman
Most rare.

CERIMON
Hush, my gentle neighbours!
Lend me your hands; to the next chamber bear her.
Get linen: now this matter must be look'd to,
For her relapse is mortal. Come, come;
And AEsculapius guide us!

Exeunt, carrying her away

Play the music! Please, give her room.
Gentlemen, this queen will live.

The warm breath of life comes from her.
She has not been in a coma for more than five hours;
look, she's starting to breathe again!

The gods,
acting through you, astonish us and make you famous forever.

She is alive; look,
her eyelids, covers for those heavenly jewels which Pericles has lost,
begin to open their bright gold edges;
the most wonderful diamonds appear, and the world is twice as rich. Live, and make us weep to hear your story, fair creature,
unique as you seem to be.

Oh dear Diana,
where am I? Where's my lord? What world am I in?

Isn't this strange?

Very unusual.

Quiet, my gentle neighbours!
Give me a hand; carry her to the next room.
Get sheets: we must treat her at once,
for a relapse would be fatal. Come on, come on;
and let the God of healing guide us.

SCENE III. Tarsus. A room in CLEON's house.

Enter PERICLES, CLEON, DIONYZA, and LYCHORIDA with MARINA in her arms

PERICLES
Most honour'd Cleon, I must needs be gone;
My twelve months are expired, and Tyrus stands
In a litigious peace. You, and your lady,
Take from my heart all thankfulness! The gods

Make up the rest upon you!

Most honoured Cleon, I have to go;
my twelve months are up, and the peace of Tyre
is disturbed with constant bickering. I thank you
and your lady from the bottom of my heart! May
the gods
make up what I'm not fit to give!

CLEON
Your shafts of fortune, though they hurt you mortally,

Yet glance full wanderingly on us.

The arrows of fate, although they have fatally
wounded you,
have also wounded us as they rebound.

DIONYZA
O your sweet queen!
That the strict fates had pleased you had brought her hither,
To have bless'd mine eyes with her!

Oh your sweet queen!
I wish the stern fates have allowed you to bring
her here,
to have delighted my sight!

PERICLES
We cannot but obey
The powers above us. Could I rage and roar
As doth the sea she lies in, yet the end
Must be as 'tis. My gentle babe Marina, whom,
For she was born at sea, I have named so, here

I charge your charity withal, leaving her
The infant of your care; beseeching you

We can only obey
the will of the gods. I could rage and roar
like the sea she is buried in, but in the end
nothing would change. My gentle baby Marina,
whom I have named after the fact that she was
born at sea,
I ask you to show your kindness to; I will leave
the child in your care; I beg you

To give her princely training, that she may be
Manner'd as she is born.

to bring her up as a princess, so that she can
have manners which fit with the status she is
born to.

CLEON
Fear not, my lord, but think
Your grace, that fed my country with your corn,

Do not worry, my lord; be assured
that you are still remembered in the people's
prayers

For which the people's prayers still fall upon you,
Must in your child be thought on. If neglection
Should therein make me vile, the common body,

for feeding my country with your corn,
and they will remember your child too. If I
was horrible enough to neglect her the common
people,

By you relieved, would force me to my duty:
But if to that my nature need a spur,
The gods revenge it upon me and mine,
To the end of generation!

whom you saved, would force me to do my duty:
but if I should ever need such a reminder,
may the gods punish me and my family for it
to the end of time!

PERICLES
I believe you;
Your honour and your goodness teach me to't,

I believe you;
your honour and goodness show me you will do
it,

Without your vows. Till she be married, madam,

without your promises. Until she is married,
madam,

By bright Diana, whom we honour, all
Unscissor'd shall this hair of mine remain,
Though I show ill in't. So I take my leave.

I swear by Diana, whom we worship, that my
hair shall remain uncut,
although it makes me look bad. And so I must
leave.

Good madam, make me blessed in your care

Good madam, give me blessings through your
care

In bringing up my child.

as you bring up my child.

DIONYZA
I have one myself,
Who shall not be more dear to my respect
Than yours, my lord.

I have a child myself,
and yours will be treated exactly
the same, my lord.

PERICLES
Madam, my thanks and prayers.

Madam, I give you my thanks and prayers.

CLEON
We'll bring your grace e'en to the edge o' the shore,

We'll go with your grace up to the edge of the
sea,

Then give you up to the mask'd Neptune and

where we'll hand you over to the now calm
Neptune and

The gentlest winds of heaven.

the gentlest winds of heaven.

PERICLES
I will embrace

I will accept

Your offer. Come, dearest madam. O, no tears,

Lychorida, no tears:
Look to your little mistress, on whose grace
You may depend hereafter. Come, my lord.

Exeunt

your offer gladly. Come, dearest madam. Oh, don't cry,
Lychordia, don't cry:
look after your little mistress, who will look after you in the future. Come, my lord.

SCENE IV. Ephesus. A room in CERIMON's house.

Enter CERIMON and THAISA

CERIMON
Madam, this letter, and some certain jewels,
Lay with you in your coffer: which are now
At your command. Know you the character?

THAISA
It is my lord's.
That I was shipp'd at sea, I well remember,
Even on my eaning time; but whether there
Deliver'd, by the holy gods,
I cannot rightly say. But since King Pericles,

My wedded lord, I ne'er shall see again,
A vestal livery will I take me to,

And never more have joy.

CERIMON
Madam, if this you purpose as ye speak,
Diana's temple is not distant far,
Where you may abide till your date expire.
Moreover, if you please, a niece of mine
Shall there attend you.

THAISA
My recompense is thanks, that's all;
Yet my good will is great, though the gift small.

Exeunt

*Madam, this letter, and some very good jewels,
were in your coffin with you: these are now
yours. Do you know the handwriting?*

*It is my husband's.
I can definitely remember going on a boat,
even though I was pregnant; but whether I gave
birth there, I swear
I cannot say for sure. But since I shall never
again see
King Pericles, my beloved husband,
I shall live the life of a handmaiden in the
temple,
and never know happiness again.*

*Madam, if you mean to do as you say,
Diana's temple is not far off,
and you can live there until your life is over.
Furthermore, if you wish it, a niece of mine
will serve you there.*

*All I can give you in return is my thanks;
but my gratitude is great, though the gift is
small.*

Act 4

SCENE I. Tarsus. An open place near the sea-shore.

Enter GOWER

GOWER
Imagine Pericles arrived at Tyre,
Welcomed and settled to his own desire.
His woeful queen we leave at Ephesus,
Unto Diana there a votaress.
Now to Marina bend your mind,
Whom our fast-growing scene must find
At Tarsus, and by Cleon train'd
In music, letters; who hath gain'd
Of education all the grace,
Which makes her both the heart and place
Of general wonder. But, alack,
That monster envy, oft the wrack
Of earned praise, Marina's life
Seeks to take off by treason's knife.
And in this kind hath our Cleon
One daughter, and a wench full grown,

Even ripe for marriage-rite; this maid
Hight Philoten: and it is said
For certain in our story, she
Would ever with Marina be:
Be't when she weaved the sleided silk
With fingers long, small, white as milk;
Or when she would with sharp needle wound
The cambric, which she made more sound

By hurting it; or when to the lute
She sung, and made the night-bird mute,
That still records with moan; or when
She would with rich and constant pen
Vail to her mistress Dian; still
This Philoten contends in skill
With absolute Marina: so
With the dove of Paphos might the crow
Vie feathers white. Marina gets
All praises, which are paid as debts,
And not as given. This so darks
In Philoten all graceful marks,
That Cleon's wife, with envy rare,
A present murderer does prepare
For good Marina, that her daughter
Might stand peerless by this slaughter.

*Now imagine Pericles has arrived at Tyre,
welcomed and following his destiny.
We leave his sad queen at Ephesus,
devoted to the worship of Diana.
Now turn your mind to Marina,
whom our quick moving show discovers
at Tarsus, trained in the study of music
by Cleon; she has taken on
all the grace she has been taught,
which makes her the very centre
of heartfelt wonder. But, alas,
the monster jealousy, which often attacks
well earned praise, tries to take
Marina's life through treason;
Cleon has another of the same kind,
one daughter, a full-grown lass, ready for
marriage.
This girl is called Philoten; and our story
tells us for certain, that she
was always with Marina:
whether when she weaved the threads of silk
with her long slender white fingers;
or when she put her sharp needle through
the fabric, which she made more beautiful
by harming it; or when she sang to the
accompaniment
of a lute, and silenced the nightingale
that is always singing sadly; or when
she would with her skilful pen write
homages to the goddess Diana; still
this Philoten tried to compete
with perfect Marina: like
a crow trying to compete with a holy dove
as to whose feathers were whitest. Marina gets
all the praise, which she fully deserved
as the wages of her virtue. This so damaged
Philoten's character and grace
that Cleon's wife with extreme jealousy
employed a murderer to attack
good Marina, so that her daughter
would have no rival after her slaughter.
To help her vile thoughts further,*

70

The sooner her vile thoughts to stead,
Lychorida, our nurse, is dead:
And cursed Dionyza hath
The pregnant instrument of wrath
Prest for this blow. The unborn event
I do commend to your content:
Only I carry winged time
Post on the lame feet of my rhyme;
Which never could I so convey,
Unless your thoughts went on my way.
Dionyza does appear,
With Leonine, a murderer.

*Lychordia, the nurse, is dead;
and cursed Dionyza has
the prepared weapon of her anger
ready to give this blow. I leave you with
this coming event; I have only tried to move
time forward with my poor speeches;
I could never manage to do this
without the help of your imagination.*

*Here is Dionyza,
with Leonine, a murderer.*

Exit

Enter DIONYZA and LEONINE

DIONYZA
Thy oath remember; thou hast sworn to do't:

*Remember your oath; you have sworn you will
do it:*

'Tis but a blow, which never shall be known.
Thou canst not do a thing in the world so soon,

*it's just a blow, and it will never be discovered.
There's not another thing in the world you could
do*

To yield thee so much profit. Let not conscience,

*that would do you so much good. Don't let
conscience,*

Which is but cold, inflaming love i' thy bosom,

*which for me is cold, start any love in your
heart,*

Inflame too nicely; nor let pity, which
Even women have cast off, melt thee, but be
A soldier to thy purpose.

*which could stop you; and don't let pity, which
even women can ignore, soften you, but stay
steadfast to your task.*

LEONINE
I will do't; but yet she is a goodly creature.

I will do it, although she is a lovely creature.

DIONYZA
The fitter, then, the gods should have her. Here
she comes weeping for her only mistress' death.
Thou art resolved?

*All the better for the gods to have her then. Here
she comes, weeping over the death of her nurse.
You are determined?*

LEONINE
I am resolved.

I am.

Enter MARINA, with a basket of flowers

MARINA
No, I will rob Tellus of her weed,
To strew thy green with flowers: the yellows, blues,

*No, I will take the clothes of the earth,
to cover your grave with flowers: the yellows,
blues,*

71

The purple violets, and marigolds,
Shall as a carpet hang upon thy grave,
While summer-days do last. Ay me! poor maid,
Born in a tempest, when my mother died,
This world to me is like a lasting storm,
Whirring me from my friends.

DIONYZA
How now, Marina! why do you keep alone?
How chance my daughter is not with you? Do not
Consume your blood with sorrowing: you have
A nurse of me. Lord, how your favour's changed
With this unprofitable woe!
Come, give me your flowers, ere the sea mar it.

Walk with Leonine; the air is quick here,
And it pierces and sharpens the stomach. Come,
Leonine, take her by the arm, walk with her.

MARINA
No, I pray you;
I'll not bereave you of your servant.

DIONYZA
Come, come;
I love the king your father, and yourself,
With more than foreign heart. We every day
Expect him here: when he shall come and find
Our paragon to all reports thus blasted,
He will repent the breadth of his great voyage;
Blame both my lord and me, that we have taken
No care to your best courses. Go, I pray you,

Walk, and be cheerful once again; reserve
That excellent complexion, which did steal
The eyes of young and old. Care not for me

I can go home alone.

MARINA
Well, I will go;
But yet I have no desire to it.

DIONYZA
Come, come, I know 'tis good for you.
Walk half an hour, Leonine, at the least:
Remember what I have said.

the purple violets, and marigolds,
shall cover your grave like a carpet,
while the summer lasts. Alas! Poor girl,
born in a storm in which my mother died,
this world to me is like a never-ending storm,
whirling me away from my friends.

Hello there, Marina! Why are you alone?
Why is my daughter not with you? Do not
give up your life to sorrow: you have
a nurse in me. Lord, how your face is changed
through this useless sorrow!
Come, give me your flowers, before the sea
spoils them.
Walk with Leonine; the air is fresh here,
and it sharpens the appetite. Come on,
Leonine, take her by the arm, walk with her.

No, please;
I don't want to take your servant away.

Come, come;
I love your father the king, and you,
as if we were related. We expect him here
very soon: when he comes and finds the one
our letters told him was so perfect so damaged,
he will regret having travelled so far;
he will be angry with my lord and me, thinking
that we have not been taking care of you. Go,
please,
walk, and be cheerful again; restore
that wonderful complexion, which attracted
the eyes of young and old. Don't worry about
me;
I can make my own way home.

Well, I will go;
however, I don't feel like it.

Come, come, I know it will do you good.
Leonine, walk for at least half an hour:
remember what I said.

LEONINE
I warrant you, madam.

I promise I will, madam.

DIONYZA
I'll leave you, my sweet lady, for a while:
Pray, walk softly, do not heat your blood:
What! I must have a care of you.

I'll leave you for a while, my sweet lady:
please, just stroll, don't get agitated:
I really must take care of you.

MARINA
My thanks, sweet madam.

Thank you, sweet madam.

Exit DIONYZA
Is this wind westerly that blows?

Is this a west wind which is blowing?

LEONINE
South-west.

South-westerly.

MARINA
When I was born, the wind was north.

When I was born, the wind came from the North.

LEONINE
Was't so?

Did it?

MARINA
My father, as nurse said, did never fear,

But cried 'Good seaman!' to the sailors, galling
His kingly hands, haling ropes;
And, clasping to the mast, endured a sea
That almost burst the deck.

My nurse told me that my father never showed
fear,
but encouraged the sailors, blistering
his royal hands, pulling on ropes;
and, hanging on to the mast, survived a sea
that almost swamped the deck.

LEONINE
When was this?

When was this?

MARINA
When I was born:
Never was waves nor wind more violent;
And from the ladder-tackle washes off
A canvas-climber. 'Ha!' says one, 'wilt out?'
And with a dropping industry they skip
From stem to stern: the boatswain whistles, and
The master calls, and trebles their confusion.

When I was born.
There was never such violent wind and waves;
and a sail rigger was washed off from
his rope ladder. "Ha!" one said, "you're off?"
And dripping wet they stuck to their work
from stem to stern: the bosun whistled, and
the captain shouted, and trebled their confusion.

LEONINE
Come, say your prayers.

Come on, say your prayers.

MARINA

What mean you?

LEONINE
If you require a little space for prayer,
I grant it: pray; but be not tedious,
For the gods are quick of ear, and I am sworn

To do my work with haste.

MARINA
Why will you kill me?

LEONINE
To satisfy my lady.

MARINA
Why would she have me kill'd?
Now, as I can remember, by my troth,
I never did her hurt in all my life:
I never spake bad word, nor did ill turn
To any living creature: believe me, la,
I never kill'd a mouse, nor hurt a fly:
I trod upon a worm against my will,
But I wept for it. How have I offended,
Wherein my death might yield her any profit,

Or my life imply her any danger?

LEONINE
My commission
Is not to reason of the deed, but do it.

MARINA
You will not do't for all the world, I hope.
You are well favour'd, and your looks foreshow
You have a gentle heart. I saw you lately,
When you caught hurt in parting two that fought:

Good sooth, it show'd well in you: do so now:
Your lady seeks my life; come you between,
And save poor me, the weaker.

LEONINE
I am sworn,
And will dispatch.

He seizes her

What do you mean?

If you need a little time to pray,
I'll allow it: pray; but don't be slow,
for the gods understand quickly, and I have sworn
to get my work over with.

Why do you want to kill me?

To please my lady.

Why does she want to kill me?
I swear, as far as I can remember,
I never did her any harm in my life:
I never spoke a bad word, or did a bad turn,
to any living creature: believe me, sir,
I never killed a mouse, or hurt a fly:
I trod on a worm by accident,
and it upset me. What have I done
that makes her think my death would be good for her,
or that my living is any threat to her?

My orders
are not to justify the deed, but to do it.

I hope you will not do it for all the world.
You are handsome, and your looks show
that you have a gentle heart. I saw you recently,
when you got hurt in stopping two others fighting:
it really was to your credit: do the same now:
your lady wants my life; come between us,
and save poor me, the weaker one.

I have sworn I'll do it,
and I'll follow through.

Enter Pirates

First Pirate
Hold, villain!

Stop, villain!

LEONINE runs away

Second Pirate
A prize! a prize!

A prize! A prize!

Third Pirate
Half-part, mates, half-part.
Come, let's have her aboard suddenly.

Half shares, mates, half shares.
come on, let's get her on board quickly.

Exeunt Pirates with MARINA

Re-enter LEONINE

LEONINE
These roguing thieves serve the great pirate Valdes;

And they have seized Marina. Let her go:
There's no hope she will return. I'll swear
she's dead,
And thrown into the sea. But I'll see further:
Perhaps they will but please themselves upon her,
Not carry her aboard. If she remain,
Whom they have ravish'd must by me be slain.

These roving thieves serve the great pirate
Valdes;
and they have seized Marina. Let her go:
she has no hope of returning. I will swear
that she is dead,
and thrown into the sea. But I'll watch them:
perhaps they will just rape her,
and not take her on board. If she stays here,
the one they have raped must be killed by me.

Exit

75

SCENE II. Mytilene. A room in a brothel.

Enter Pandar, Bawd, and BOULT

Pandar
Boult!

Boult!

BOULT
Sir?

Sir?

Pandar
Search the market narrowly; Mytilene is full of

gallants. We lost too much money this mart by being

too wenchless.

Search the slave market carefully; Mytilene is full of
randy young men. We lost too much money this market day
through not having enough girls.

Bawd
We were never so much out of creatures. We have but

poor three, and they can do no more than they can

do; and they with continual action are even as good as
rotten.

We never had such a shortage of them. We've only got
three poor ones, and they can't do more than they are;
and with continuous work they're pretty much worn out.

Pandar
Therefore let's have fresh ones, whate'er we pay for

them. If there be not a conscience to be used in

every trade, we shall never prosper.

So let's get some fresh ones, whatever we have to pay
for them. If we don't follow good business principles,
we'll never turn a profit.

Bawd
Thou sayest true: 'tis not our bringing up of poor

bastards,--as, I think, I have brought up some eleven--

You speak the truth: it's not the way we raise the poor
bastards–I think I've brought up about eleven—

BOULT
Ay, to eleven; and brought them down again. But

shall I search the market?

Yes, to the age of eleven, and then ruined them again.
But shall I search the market?

Bawd
What else, man? The stuff we have, a strong wind

will blow it to pieces, they are so pitifully sodden.

What else can we do, man? This stuff we have, a strong wind
would blow to pieces, they are soaked through.

Pandar
Thou sayest true; they're too unwholesome, o'

conscience. The poor Transylvanian is dead, that
lay with the little baggage.

You're telling the truth; they are riddled with disease,
to be honest. The poor Transylvanian is dead
the one who slept with the little baggage.

BOULT
Ay, she quickly pooped him; she made him roast-meat

for worms. But I'll go search the market.

Yes, she quickly ruined him; she made him a dinner
for the worms. But I'll go and search the market.

Exit

Pandar
Three or four thousand chequins were as pretty a

proportion to live quietly, and so give over.

Three or four thousand gold coins would be a nice
nest egg for a quiet life, so one could retire.

Bawd
Why to give over, I pray you? is it a shame to get

when we are old?

Why retire, may I ask? Is it shameful to still make
money when we are old?

Pandar
O, our credit comes not in like the commodity, nor

the commodity wages not with the danger: therefore,
if in our youths we could pick up some pretty
estate, 'twere not amiss to keep our door hatched.

Besides, the sore terms we stand upon with the gods
will be strong with us for giving over.

Oh, we don't get credit in the same way as we get profits,
the two do not match each other: therefore,
if when we are young we can pick up some nice
property, it wouldn't be a bad thing to close
down the business.
Besides, the bad standing we have with the gods
is a good reason to pack it in.

Bawd
Come, other sorts offend as well as we.

Come now, there are others who are just as bad as us.

Pandar
As well as we! ay, and better too; we offend worse.

Neither is our profession any trade; it's no
calling. But here comes Boult.

As bad as us! Yes and better ones; we are the worst offenders.
And our profession is not a trade; it's not
a calling. But here comes Boult.

Re-enter BOULT, with the Pirates and MARINA

BOULT
[To MARINA] Come your ways. My masters, you say

Come along. My masters, you say

77

she's a virgin?

she is a virgin?

First Pirate
O, sir, we doubt it not.

No doubt about it, sir.

BOULT
Master, I have gone through for this piece, you see:
if you like her, so; if not, I have lost my earnest.

*Master, I have made a deal for this piece here:
if you like her, good; if not, I have lost my
deposit.*

Bawd
Boult, has she any qualities?

Boult, does she have any accomplishments?

BOULT
She has a good face, speaks well, and has excellent
good clothes: there's no further necessity of
qualities can make her be refused.

*She has a good face, speaks well, and has very
good clothes: no lack of accomplishment
would be grounds for turning her down.*

Bawd
What's her price, Boult?

How much is she, Boult?

BOULT
I cannot be bated one doit of a thousand pieces.

*I can't get her for a cent less than a thousand
gold pieces.*

Pandar
Well, follow me, my masters, you shall have your
money presently. Wife, take her in; instruct her
what she has to do, that she may not be raw in her

entertainment.

*Well, follow me, my masters, you will have your
money shortly. Wife, take her inside; show her
what she has to do, so that she won't be
inexperienced
when she starts work.*

Exeunt Pandar and Pirates

Bawd
Boult, take you the marks of her, the colour of her

hair, complexion, height, age, with warrant of her

virginity; and cry 'He that will give most shall

have her first.' Such a maidenhead were no cheap

thing, if men were as they have been. Get this done
as I command you.

*Boult, you make a note of her appearance, the
colour of her
hair, complexion, height, age, and her
guaranteed
virginity; go and announce, 'Whoever pays the
most
will have her first.' Such virginity will fetch a
good
price, if men are the same as ever. Do as I
tell you.*

BOULT
Performance shall follow.

I shall do so.

78

Exit

MARINA
Alack that Leonine was so slack, so slow!
He should have struck, not spoke; or that these pirates,

Not enough barbarous, had not o'erboard thrown me

For to seek my mother!

Bawd
Why lament you, pretty one?

MARINA
That I am pretty.

Bawd
Come, the gods have done their part in you.

MARINA
I accuse them not.

Bawd
You are light into my hands, where you are like to live.

MARINA
The more my fault
To scape his hands where I was like to die.

Bawd
Ay, and you shall live in pleasure.

MARINA
No.

Bawd
Yes, indeed shall you, and taste gentlemen of all

fashions: you shall fare well; you shall have the
difference of all complexions. What! do you stop your
ears?

MARINA
Are you a woman?

Alas that Leonine was so neglectful, so slow!
He should have stabbed me, not spoken; and alas
that these pirates were not more barbarous, that they
didn't throw me overboard to find my mother!

Why are you so sad, pretty one?

Because I am pretty.

Come now, the gods have favoured you.

I don't blame them.

You have fallen into my hands, which is where you are going to live.

The worse luck for me
that I escaped the hands whereby I was going to die.

Yes, and you will have a life of pleasure.

No.

Yes, you certainly will, and sample gentlemen of all
types: you will do well; you'll have men of every race. What's this! Are you blocking your ears?

Are you a woman?

Bawd
What would you have me be, an I be not a woman?

What do you think I am, if I'm not a woman?

MARINA
An honest woman, or not a woman.

If you're not honest, you're not a woman.

Bawd
Marry, whip thee, gosling: I think I shall have
something to do with you. Come, you're a young

foolish sapling, and must be bowed as I would have
you.

*Why, be damned to you, greenhorn: I can see
I'll have trouble with you. Come on, you're
a young
foolish sapling, and I shall have to bend you
to the shape I desire.*

MARINA
The gods defend me!

May the gods defend me!

Bawd
If it please the gods to defend you by men, then men

must comfort you, men must feed you, men must stir
you up. Boult's returned.

*If the gods decide to defend you through men,
then men
must comfort you, men must feed you, men must
get you going. Boult's back.*

Re-enter BOULT
Now, sir, hast thou cried her through the market?

Now, sir, have you advertised her in the market?

BOULT
I have cried her almost to the number of her hairs;

I have drawn her picture with my voice.

*I have described her as minutely as you could
wish;
I have painted a picture of her with my voice.*

Bawd
And I prithee tell me, how dost thou find the

inclination of the people, especially of the younger sort?

*So please, tell me, what sort of interest did you
get
from the people, particularly the younger ones?*

BOULT
'Faith, they listened to me as they would have

hearkened to their father's testament. There was a
Spaniard's mouth so watered, that he went to bed to

her very description.

*By God, they listened to me as closely as they
would have
listened to their father's will. There was a
Spaniard who was so hungry for her, he was
almost
sleeping with her description.*

Bawd
We shall have him here to-morrow with his best ruff on.

He'll be here tomorrow in his best outfit.

BOULT
To-night, to-night. But, mistress, do you know the

Tonight, tonight. But, mistress, you know the

80

French knight that cowers i' the hams?

French knight, the diseased one?

Bawd
Who, Monsieur Veroles?

Who, Monsieur Veroles?

BOULT
Ay, he: he offered to cut a caper at the proclamation; but he made a groan at it, and swore he would see her to-morrow.

Yes, him: he danced with excitement at the announcement; then he gave a groan, and swore he would see her tomorrow.

Bawd
Well, well; as for him, he brought his disease hither: here he does but repair it. I know he will come in our shadow, to scatter his crowns in the

sun.

Good, good; as for him, he brought his disease with him: he just tops it up here. I know he will come into our house, and chuck his money around.

BOULT
Well, if we had of every nation a traveller, we

should lodge them with this sign.

Well, if we had a traveller from every nation on earth,
they would all want to have a go at her.

Bawd
[To MARINA] Pray you, come hither awhile. You have fortunes coming upon you. Mark me: you must

seem to do that fearfully which you commit willingly, despise profit where you have most gain.

To weep that you live as ye do makes pity in your

lovers: seldom but that pity begets you a good opinion, and that opinion a mere profit.

Now you, come here for a moment. You have a fortune coming to you. Mark my words: you must
pretend that you are reluctant to do what you do willingly, and to hate the profits even as you make them.
You must weep about your life, which will create pity
in your lovers: it's not often that pity gets you goodwill, and that goodwill will be sheer profit.

MARINA
I understand you not.

I don't understand you.

BOULT
O, take her home, mistress, take her home: these blushes of hers must be quenched with some present practise.

Oh, take her home, mistress take her home: this shyness must be knocked out of her with practice.

Bawd
Thou sayest true, i' faith, so they must; for your bride goes to that with shame which is her way to go with warrant.

By God you're telling the truth, it must; the bride goes with shame to the thing that it is lawful for her to do.

BOULT

'Faith, some do, and some do not. But, mistress, if
I have bargained for the joint,--

*Well, some do and some do not. But, mistress, as
I have prepared the joint—*

Bawd
Thou mayst cut a morsel off the spit.

Yes, you can have a slice.

BOULT
I may so.

I will do so.

Bawd
Who should deny it? Come, young one, I like the

manner of your garments well.

*Who would refuse it you? Come on, young one, I
like
the cut of your clothes.*

BOULT
Ay, by my faith, they shall not be changed yet.

Yes, by God, they shall not be changed yet.

Bawd
Boult, spend thou that in the town: report what a
sojourner we have; you'll lose nothing by custom.

When nature framed this piece, she meant thee a good
turn; therefore say what a paragon she is, and thou

hast the harvest out of thine own report.

*Boult, tell it all round the town: report who
we have staying here; you'll get a profit from the
customers.
When nature made this girl, she did you a good
turn; so tell everyone how wonderful she is, and
you
will get a reward from your reports.*

BOULT
I warrant you, mistress, thunder shall not so awake
the beds of eels as my giving out her beauty stir up
the lewdly-inclined. I'll bring home some to-night.

*I guarantee you, mistress, the dirty minded
will be more excited by my reports of her beauty
than a bed of eels stirred up by a storm. I'll
bring some home tonight.*

Bawd
Come your ways; follow me.

Come along; follow me.

MARINA
If fires be hot, knives sharp, or waters deep,

Untied I still my virgin knot will keep.
Diana, aid my purpose!

*If I can find a hot fire, a sharp knife, or deep
water,
I shall preserve my virginity.
Diana, help me!*

Bawd
What have we to do with Diana? Pray you, will you
go with us?

*What's Diana got to do with us? You just come
along with me.*

Exeunt

82

SCENE III. Tarsus. A room in CLEON's house.

Enter CLEON and DIONYZA

DIONYZA
Why are you foolish? Can it be undone?

Why are you being so stupid? Can it be changed?

CLEON
O Dionyza, such a piece of slaughter
The sun and moon ne'er look'd upon!

Oh Dionyza, there was never such a murder in the history of the world!

DIONYZA
I think
You'll turn a child again.

I think you're becoming like a child again.

CLEON
Were I chief lord of all this spacious world,
I'd give it to undo the deed. O lady,
Much less in blood than virtue, yet a princess

To equal any single crown o' the earth
I' the justice of compare! O villain Leonine!
Whom thou hast poison'd too:
If thou hadst drunk to him, 't had been a kindness

Becoming well thy fact: what canst thou say
When noble Pericles shall demand his child?

If I ruled the whole wide world, I'd give it up to undo this deed. Oh lady, you were a princess, even more through your virtues than your birth, who could stand comparison with any king on earth! Leonine, you villain! And now you have poisoned him too: if you had drunk his health with that poison it would have been an act which suited your deed: what will you say when noble Pericles asks for his child?

DIONYZA
That she is dead. Nurses are not the fates,
To foster it, nor ever to preserve.
She died at night; I'll say so. Who can cross it?

Unless you play the pious innocent,
And for an honest attribute cry out
'She died by foul play.'

I'll tell him she is dead. Nurses are not the fates, who have the power of life and death. She died at night; that's what I'll say. Who can contradict it? Unless you want to be a pious innocent, and so you'll be thought of as honest cry out, 'She died of foul play.'

CLEON
O, go to. Well, well,
Of all the faults beneath the heavens, the gods
Do like this worst.

Oh, get lost. Well, well, of all the faults of mankind, the gods hate this the most.

DIONYZA
Be one of those that think
The petty wrens of Tarsus will fly hence,
And open this to Pericles. I do shame

You're one of those who thinks that the little birds of Tarsus will fly away and reveal the truth to Pericles. I'm ashamed

To think of what a noble strain you are,
And of how coward a spirit.

to think what a noble family you come from,
when you have such a cowardly spirit.

CLEON
To such proceeding
Who ever but his approbation added,
Though not his prime consent, he did not flow

From honourable sources.

Anybody who ever approved
such an act,
even though he wasn't directly involved, he did not
come from honourable ancestry.

DIONYZA
Be it so, then:
Yet none does know, but you, how she came dead,
Nor none can know, Leonine being gone.
She did disdain my child, and stood between
Her and her fortunes: none would look on her,
But cast their gazes on Marina's face;
Whilst ours was blurted at and held a malkin
Not worth the time of day. It pierced me through;

And though you call my course unnatural,
You not your child well loving, yet I find
It greets me as an enterprise of kindness
Perform'd to your sole daughter.

So be it, then:
but nobody knows how she died apart from you,
and nobody can know, now that Leonine is dead.
She outshone my child, and stood between
her and her fortunes: nobody would look at her,
they all looked at Marina instead;
our child was sneered at and thought a slut
who was not worth the time of day. It stabbed
me to the heart;
and though you call my actions unnatural,
as you don't love your child enough, for me
this was an act of kindness, performed
for the sake of your only daughter.

CLEON
Heavens forgive it!

May heaven forgive it!

DIONYZA
And as for Pericles,
What should he say? We wept after her hearse,
And yet we mourn: her monument
Is almost finish'd, and her epitaphs
In glittering golden characters express
A general praise to her, and care in us
At whose expense 'tis done.

And as for Pericles,
what's he going to say? We wept at her funeral,
and we are still in mourning: her monument
is almost finished, and her epitaphs
show great praise for her
in glittering golden letters, and they show
how much we cared, the ones who paid for it.

CLEON
Thou art like the harpy,
Which, to betray, dost, with thine angel's face,

Seize with thine eagle's talons.

You are like the harpy,
which traps people by showing the face of an angel
whilst grabbing them with the claws of an eagle.

DIONYZA
You are like one that superstitiously

And you are like one who is so scared of the gods

Doth swear to the gods that winter kills the flies:

But yet I know you'll do as I advise.

Exeunt

that you have to swear to them that winter killed
the flies, not you:
and yet I know you'll do as I say.

SCENE IV.

Enter GOWER, before the monument of MARINA at Tarsus

GOWER
Thus time we waste, and longest leagues make short;

Sail seas in cockles, have an wish but for't;

Making, to take your imagination,
From bourn to bourn, region to region.
By you being pardon'd, we commit no crime
To use one language in each several clime

Where our scenes seem to live. I do beseech you
To learn of me, who stand i' the gaps to teach you,
The stages of our story. Pericles
Is now again thwarting the wayward seas,
Attended on by many a lord and knight.
To see his daughter, all his life's delight.
Old Escanes, whom Helicanus late
Advanced in Tyre to great and high estate,
Is left to govern. Bear you it in mind,
Old Helicanus goes along behind.
Well-sailing ships and bounteous winds have brought

This king to Tarsus,--think his pilot thought;
So with his steerage shall your thoughts grow on,--
To fetch his daughter home, who first is gone.

Like motes and shadows see them move awhile;

Your ears unto your eyes I'll reconcile.

And so we make time fly past, and telescope distances;

we can sail the seas in seashells, just because we want to;

travelling through our imagination from border to border, country to country. If you forgive us, there is no crime to use a single language for the different countries

where our scene seems to be set. I now ask you to listen to me, whose job is to fill in the gaps in our story. Pericles is once again crossing the dangerous seas, accompanied by many lords and knights, to see his daughter, the great joy of his life. Old Helicanus goes with him. They have left old Escanes behind to govern, please note that; Helicanus recently promoted him to a high position in Tyre. Fast running ships and friendly winds have brought

this king to Tarsus–keep this thought in mind, so you remember it as his journey goes on– To bring his daughter home, who has already left.

Watch them move for you in dumb show for a while;

afterwards I'll explain to you what you've seen.

DUMB SHOW.

Enter PERICLES, at one door, with all his train; CLEON and DIONYZA, at the other. CLEON shows PERICLES the tomb; whereat PERICLES makes lamentation, puts on sackcloth, and in a mighty passion departs. Then exeunt CLEON and DIONYZA

See how belief may suffer by foul show!
This borrow'd passion stands for true old woe;

And Pericles, in sorrow all devour'd,
With sighs shot through, and biggest tears
o'ershower'd,
Leaves Tarsus and again embarks. He swears

See how belief can suffer through hypocrisy! This counterfeit passion stands in for real sorrow;

and Pericles, overcome with sorrow, racked with sighs and swamped with tears, leaves Tarsus and re-embarks. He swears

Never to wash his face, nor cut his hairs:

He puts on sackcloth, and to sea. He bears
A tempest, which his mortal vessel tears,
And yet he rides it out. Now please you wit.
The epitaph is for Marina writ
By wicked Dionyza.

Reads the inscription on MARINA's monument
'The fairest, sweet'st, and best lies here,
Who wither'd in her spring of year.
She was of Tyrus the king's daughter,
On whom foul death hath made this slaughter;

Marina was she call'd; and at her birth,

Thetis, being proud, swallow'd some part o' the earth:

Therefore the earth, fearing to be o'erflow'd,
Hath Thetis' birth-child on the heavens bestow'd:
Wherefore she does, and swears she'll never stint,
Make raging battery upon shores of flint.'
No visor does become black villany
So well as soft and tender flattery.
Let Pericles believe his daughter's dead,
And bear his courses to be ordered
By Lady Fortune; while our scene must play
His daughter's woe and heavy well-a-day
In her unholy service. Patience, then,
And think you now are all in Mytilene.

Exit

that he shall never wash his face not cut his hair again.
He puts on sackcloth, and sets out to sea. He has encountered a storm, which tears at his body, and yet he survives it. Now you should know that this epitaph is written for Marina by the wicked Dionyza.

'The fairest, sweetest and best, lies here, who died while still in her youth.
She was the daughter of the king of Tyre, whom foul death has attacked with this slaughter.
She was called Marina; when she was born the god of the sea
proud that she was born in his domain, took the part of the earth.
So the earth, fearing it would be flooded, has sent his child up to heaven;
where she makes endless attacks upon the flinty shores.
No mask suits black villainy as well as soft and tender flattery.
Let Pericles believe his daughter is dead, and think his life is ordered
by the fates; meanwhile we must show his daughter's sorrow and heavy grief in her devilish service. Indulge us, then, and now imagine you are all in Mytilen.

SCENE V. Mytilene. A street before the brothel.

Enter, from the brothel, two Gentlemen

First Gentleman
Did you ever hear the like?

Did you ever hear anything like it?

Second Gentleman
No, nor never shall do in such a place as this, she being once gone.

No, nor will I ever do in a place like this, once she is gone.

First Gentleman
But to have divinity preached there! did you ever

dream of such a thing?

But to have divinity preached in a brothel! Did you
ever think such a thing could happen?

Second Gentleman
No, no. Come, I am for no more bawdy-houses:

shall's go hear the vestals sing?

Certainly not. Come, I'll stay out of brothels
from now on:
shall we go to hear the temple virgins singing?

First Gentleman
I'll do anything now that is virtuous; but I am out of the road of rutting for ever.

I'll do anything that is good now; but I
have finished with randy behaviour forever.

Exeunt

SCENE VI. The same. A room in the brothel.

Enter Pandar, Bawd, and BOULT

Pandar
Well, I had rather than twice the worth of her she

had ne'er come here.

Well, I would have given twice what I paid for
her
for her never to have come here.

Bawd
Fie, fie upon her! she's able to freeze the god

Priapus, and undo a whole generation. We must either get her ravished, or be rid of her. When she

should do for clients her fitment, and do me the

kindness of our profession, she has me her quirks,

her reasons, her master reasons, her prayers, her knees; that she would make a puritan of the devil,

Damn her, damn her! She's been able to beat
down
Priapus, and ruin a whole generation. We must
either have her raped, or get rid of her. When
she
should be entertaining the clients, and obeying
me
as my employee, she gives me her
idiosyncrasies,
her reasons, her great reasons, her prayers, her
kneeling; if the devil tried to get a kiss from her

if he should cheapen a kiss of her.

she would turn him into a puritan.

BOULT
'Faith, I must ravish her, or she'll disfurnish us
of all our cavaliers, and make our swearers priests.

*By God, I must rape her, or she'll put off all
our young gentleman, and turn our regulars into
priests.*

Pandar
Now, the pox upon her green-sickness for me!

*Now, I say a pox upon her inexperienced
innocence!*

Bawd
'Faith, there's no way to be rid on't but by the

way to the pox. Here comes the Lord Lysimachus
disguised.

*By God, there's no way we can get rid of it
except by
the method which gives you the pox. Here comes
Lord Lysimachus disguised.*

BOULT
We should have both lord and lown, if the peevish

baggage would but give way to customers.

*We would have Lords and the lowborn coming,
if the sullen
baggage would just let the customers have a go
at her.*

Enter LYSIMACHUS

LYSIMACHUS
How now! How a dozen of virginities?

Hello there! What price for a dozen virginities?

Bawd
Now, the gods to-bless your honour!

Now, may the gods bless your honour!

BOULT
I am glad to see your honour in good health.

I'm glad to see your honour is in good health.

LYSIMACHUS
You may so; 'tis the better for you that your
resorters stand upon sound legs. How now!
wholesome iniquity have you that a man may deal

withal, and defy the surgeon?

*I'm sure you are; it's better for you if your
customers are healthy. Well now!
Have you got some healthy bit of sin to offer a
chap,
so that he wouldn't have to see the doctor
afterwards?*

Bawd
We have here one, sir, if she would--but there never

came her like in Mytilene.

*We do have one like that, sir, if she would give
in—but
no one like her ever came to Mytilene.*

LYSIMACHUS

89

If she'ld do the deed of darkness, thou wouldst say.

If she would do the deeds of darkness, as you would call them.

Bawd
Your honour knows what 'tis to say well enough.

Your honour knows what they're called well enough.

LYSIMACHUS
Well, call forth, call forth.

Well bring her out, bring her out.

BOULT
For flesh and blood, sir, white and red, you shall
see a rose; and she were a rose indeed, if she had but--

For physical presence, sir, pink and white, you will see a rose; and she would be a rose indeed, if she only had–

LYSIMACHUS
What, prithee?

What, tell me.

BOULT
O, sir, I can be modest.

No, sir, I will be polite.

LYSIMACHUS
That dignifies the renown of a bawd, no less than it
gives a good report to a number to be chaste.

Well, that makes a pimp look better, just as it does for plenty of those who are supposedly pure.

Exit BOULT

Bawd
Here comes that which grows to the stalk; never

plucked yet, I can assure you.

Here comes the one that grows on the stalk; never
yet plucked, I can promise you.

Re-enter BOULT with MARINA
Is she not a fair creature?

Isn't it a beautiful creature?

LYSIMACHUS
'Faith, she would serve after a long voyage at sea.
Well, there's for you: leave us.

Well, she would do for after a long sea voyage.
Well, there's your fee: leave us alone.

Bawd
I beseech your honour, give me leave: a word, and

I'll have done presently.

I beg your honour, just a moment: let me have a
word, and
I'll be finished shortly

LYSIMACHUS
I beseech you, do.

You had better.

Bawd
[To MARINA] First, I would have you note, this is an honourable man.

Firstly, I want you to note, that this is an honourable man.

MARINA
I desire to find him so, that I may worthily note him.

I hope that I will find he is, so he will be worthy of me noting him.

Bawd
Next, he's the governor of this country, and a man

whom I am bound to.

Next, he's the governor of this country, and the man who rules over me.

MARINA
If he govern the country, you are bound to him

indeed; but how honourable he is in that, I know not.

If he governs the country, you are certainly ruled by him; but how honourable that makes him, I don't know.

Bawd
Pray you, without any more virginal fencing, will

you use him kindly? He will line your apron with gold.

Now can you please, without any more virginal resistance, treat him well? He will fill your apron with gold.

MARINA
What he will do graciously, I will thankfully receive.

Whatever he does politely, I will welcome with thanks.

LYSIMACHUS
Ha' you done?

Have you finished?

Bawd
My lord, she's not paced yet: you must take some

pains to work her to your manage. Come, we will

leave his honour and her together. Go thy ways.

My Lord, she's not broken yet: you will have to make some efforts before you can ride her. Come on, we will leave them together. Go about your business.

Exeunt Bawd, Pandar, and BOULT

LYSIMACHUS
Now, pretty one, how long have you been at this trade?

Now, pretty one, how long have you been in this business?

MARINA
What trade, sir?

What business, sir?

LYSIMACHUS
Why, I cannot name't but I shall offend.

Why, I can't name it without being rude.

MARINA
I cannot be offended with my trade. Please you to name it.

I can't be offended by the name of my trade. Please name it.

LYSIMACHUS
How long have you been of this profession?

How long have you been in this profession?

MARINA
E'er since I can remember.

Ever since I can remember.

LYSIMACHUS
Did you go to 't so young? Were you a gamester at five or at seven?

Did you start off so young? Were you a tart at five or seven?

MARINA
Earlier too, sir, if now I be one.

Earlier than that, sir, if that's what I am now.

LYSIMACHUS
Why, the house you dwell in proclaims you to be a creature of sale.

Why, the house you live in advertises you as a creature who can be bought.

MARINA
Do you know this house to be a place of such resort, and will come into 't? I hear say you are of

honourable parts, and are the governor of this place.

So you know that this house is that sort of place, and you want to come inside? I've heard tell that you are an honourable man, and are the governor of this place.

LYSIMACHUS
Why, hath your principal made known unto you who I am?

Why, has your boss told you who I am?

MARINA
Who is my principal?

Who's my boss?

LYSIMACHUS
Why, your herb-woman; she that sets seeds and roots

of shame and iniquity. O, you have heard something

of my power, and so stand aloof for more serious

wooing. But I protest to thee, pretty one, my

authority shall not see thee, or else look friendly

Why, that gardener; the one that puts down the seeds and roots of shame and disgrace. I see, you have heard about my power, and so you're being standoffish, hoping for a better proposal. But I must tell you, pretty one, I can't see you in an official capacity, or otherwise be

92

upon thee. Come, bring me to some private place:
come, come.

MARINA
If you were born to honour, show it now;
If put upon you, make the judgment good
That thought you worthy of it.

LYSIMACHUS
How's this? how's this? Some more; be sage.

MARINA
For me,
That am a maid, though most ungentle fortune
Have placed me in this sty, where, since I came,
Diseases have been sold dearer than physic,

O, that the gods
Would set me free from this unhallow'd place,
Though they did change me to the meanest bird

That flies i' the purer air!

LYSIMACHUS
I did not think
Thou couldst have spoke so well; ne'er dream'd thou
couldst.
Had I brought hither a corrupted mind,
Thy speech had alter'd it. Hold, here's gold for thee:

Persever in that clear way thou goest,
And the gods strengthen thee!

MARINA
The good gods preserve you!

LYSIMACHUS
For me, be you thoughten
That I came with no ill intent; for to me
The very doors and windows savour vilely.
Fare thee well. Thou art a piece of virtue, and
I doubt not but thy training hath been noble.

Hold, here's more gold for thee.
A curse upon him, die he like a thief,

friendly
to you. Come on, take me somewhere private:
come on, come on.

If you have any natural honour, show it now;
if you have any honour that's been given to you,
justify the faith of those who thought you were
worth it.

What's this? What's this? Say some more; be
wise.

I'll say for me,
that I am a virgin, although the cruellest fate
has put me in this pigsty, where, since I arrived,
people get diseases, paying a higher price than
they would for medicine,
oh, I wish the gods
would set me free from this unholy place,
even if it meant changing into the most
insignificant bird
that flies through the purer air!

I didn't think
that you would be able to speak so well; I never
dreamt that you could.
If I came here with a perverted mind,
your speech has changed it. Wait, here's money
for you:
keep on the straight path you're travelling,
and may the gods give you strength!

May be good gods preserve you!

For me, be assured
that I came with no bad intent; for me
the actual doors and windows revolt me.
Goodbye. You are an exemplar of virtue, and
I cannot doubt that you have been well brought
up.
Wait, here is more gold for you.
A curse on the one who robs you of your

That robs thee of thy goodness! If thou dost
Hear from me, it shall be for thy good.

goodness,
may he die like a thief! If you
hear from me, it will be for your benefit.

Re-enter BOULT

BOULT
I beseech your honour, one piece for me.

I beg your honour, a coin for me.

LYSIMACHUS
Avaunt, thou damned door-keeper!
Your house, but for this virgin that doth prop it,

Would sink and overwhelm you. Away!

Get out, you dammed doorkeeper!
Your house would sink into the mud and drown
you,
if it wasn't for this virgin holding it up. Get lost!

Exit

BOULT
How's this? We must take another course with you.

If your peevish chastity, which is not worth a

breakfast in the cheapest country under the cope,

shall undo a whole household, let me be gelded like

a spaniel. Come your ways.

What's this? We must do something else with
you.
If your sullen chastity, which is worth less than
the
price of a breakfast in the cheapest country in
the world,
is going to be allowed to bring down the whole
household,
let me be castrated like a spaniel. Come along.

MARINA
Whither would you have me?

What are you going to do to me?

BOULT
I must have your maidenhead taken off, or the common
hangman shall execute it. Come your ways. We'll
have no more gentlemen driven away. Come your
ways, I say.

I'm going to have your virginity, or the public
hangman can have it. Come along. We'll
have no more gentlemen driven away. Come
along, I say.

Re-enter Bawd

Bawd
How now! what's the matter?

What's all this! What's the matter?

BOULT
Worse and worse, mistress; she has here spoken holy

words to the Lord Lysimachus.

It gets worse and worse, mistress; she's been
speaking holy
words to the Lord Lysimachus.

Bawd

O abominable!

That's terrible!

BOULT
She makes our profession as it were to stink afore
the face of the gods.

*She makes our profession look as if it stinks
to high heaven.*

Bawd
Marry, hang her up for ever!

Well, hang her up forever!

BOULT
The nobleman would have dealt with her like a
nobleman, and she sent him away as cold as a

snowball; saying his prayers too.

*The nobleman would have treated her like a
nobleman does, and she sent him away as cold
as a
snowball; saying his prayers as well.*

Bawd
Boult, take her away; use her at thy pleasure:
crack the glass of her virginity, and make the rest
malleable.

*Boult, take her away; have your way with her:
tear through her virginity, and make her
obedient.*

BOULT
An if she were a thornier piece of ground than she
is, she shall be ploughed.

*I shall plough her, even if she was a rougher
field than she is.*

MARINA
Hark, hark, you gods!

Listen, listen, you gods!

Bawd
She conjures: away with her! Would she had never

come within my doors! Marry, hang you! She's born

to undo us. Will you not go the way of women-kind?

Marry, come up, my dish of chastity with rosemary and
bays!

*She summons: take her away! I wish she had
never
darkened my doors! Well, hang you! She was
born
to be our downfall. Why can't you do what other
women do?
Away you go, you prissy piece of virtue!*

Exit

BOULT
Come, mistress; come your ways with me.

Come, mistress; come along with me.

MARINA
Whither wilt thou have me?

What are you going to do with me?

BOULT
To take from you the jewel you hold so dear.

To take away the jewel that you find so precious.

MARINA
Prithee, tell me one thing first.

Please, tell me one thing first.

BOULT
Come now, your one thing.

Come on then, your one thing.

MARINA
What canst thou wish thine enemy to be?

What would you like the devil to be?

BOULT
Why, I could wish him to be my master, or rather,
my mistress.

*Well, I would like him to be my master, or
rather, my mistress.*

MARINA
Neither of these are so bad as thou art,
Since they do better thee in their command.
Thou hold'st a place, for which the pained'st fiend

Of hell would not in reputation change:
Thou art the damned doorkeeper to every
Coistrel that comes inquiring for his Tib;
To the choleric fisting of every rogue
Thy ear is liable; thy food is such
As hath been belch'd on by infected lungs.

*Neither of those are so bad as you are,
since at least they are in charge.
You have a position which the most tortured
daemon
of hell would not trade you for;
you are the dammed door opener for every
scoundrel that comes looking for a strumpet;
any scumbag who fancies it can box
your ears; your food is stuff
which has been belched on with infected lungs.*

BOULT
What would you have me do? go to the wars, would
you? where a man may serve seven years for the loss

of a leg, and have not money enough in the end to

buy him a wooden one?

*What you want me to do? Do you think I should
go to the wars? Where a man can serve seven
years,
lose his leg, and not have enough money at the
end of it all
to buy a wooden one?*

MARINA
Do any thing but this thou doest. Empty
Old receptacles, or common shores, of filth;
Serve by indenture to the common hangman:
Any of these ways are yet better than this;
For what thou professest, a baboon, could he speak,

Would own a name too dear. O, that the gods

Would safely deliver me from this place!
Here, here's gold for thee.
If that thy master would gain by thee,
Proclaim that I can sing, weave, sew, and dance,
With other virtues, which I'll keep from boast:

*Do anything but what you're doing now. Empty
chamber pots, or clean the common sewers;
become an apprentice to the common hangman:
any of those things are better than doing this;
what you do for a job, a baboon, if he could
speak,
would say it was beneath his dignity. Oh, I wish
the gods
would get me safely away from this place!
Here, here's gold for you.
If your master wants to make a profit from me,
advertise that I can sing, weave, sew and dance,
with other accomplishments, which I won't boast
about;*

And I will undertake all these to teach.
I doubt not but this populous city will
Yield many scholars.

BOULT
But can you teach all this you speak of?

MARINA
Prove that I cannot, take me home again,
And prostitute me to the basest groom
That doth frequent your house.

BOULT
Well, I will see what I can do for thee: if I can
place thee, I will.

MARINA
But amongst honest women.

BOULT
'Faith, my acquaintance lies little amongst them.
But since my master and mistress have bought you,

there's no going but by their consent: therefore I
will make them acquainted with your purpose, and I
doubt not but I shall find them tractable enough.
Come, I'll do for thee what I can; come your ways.

Exeunt

and I will agree to teach all of this.
I don't doubt that this crowded city will
provide many students.

But can you teach all these things you mention?

If it's shown that I cannot, bring me back here,
and sell me to the lowest groom
who comes to your house.

Well, I will see what I can do for you: if I can
find you a place, I will.

But amongst honest women.

By God, I don't know many of them.
But since my master and mistress have bought you,
you can't go without their agreement: so I
will tell them what you want to do, and I
am sure that they will be agreeable enough.
Come on, I'll do what I can for you; come along
with me.

Act 5

SCENE I. On board PERICLES' ship, off Mytilene.

A close pavilion on deck, with a curtain before it; PERICLES
within it, reclined on a couch. A barge lying
beside the Tyrian vessel.

Enter GOWER

GOWER

Marina thus the brothel 'scapes, and chances
Into an honest house, our story says.
She sings like one immortal, and she dances
As goddess-like to her admired lays;
Deep clerks she dumbs; and with her needle composes

Nature's own shape, of bud, bird, branch, or berry,

That even her art sisters the natural roses;

Her inkle, silk, twin with the rubied cherry:
That pupils lacks she none of noble race,
Who pour their bounty on her; and her gain
She gives the cursed bawd. Here we her place;

And to her father turn our thoughts again,

Where we left him, on the sea. We there him lost;
Whence, driven before the winds, he is arrived

Here where his daughter dwells; and on this coast

Suppose him now at anchor. The city strived

God Neptune's annual feast to keep: from whence
Lysimachus our Tyrian ship espies,
His banners sable, trimm'd with rich expense;
And to him in his barge with fervor hies.
In your supposing once more put your sight
Of heavy Pericles; think this his bark:
Where what is done in action, more, if might,
Shall be discover'd; please you, sit and hark.

*And so, our story says that Marina escapes
the brothel and comes into an honest house.
She sings like a goddess, and she dances
just as divinely to her lovely songs.
She does complex embroidery, and with her
needle
constructs nature's own shapes, buds, birds,
branches or berries,
that through her skill are the sisters of the
natural roses;
her silken thread is the twin of the glossy cherry:
she has plenty of pupils from the nobility,
who heap their riches upon her; and she gives
her profits to the cursed brothel keeper. We'll
leave her there
and turn our thoughts back to her father, where
we left him on the sea.*

Driven by the winds, he has arrived

*at the place where his daughter lives; now
imagine*

*that he has anchored off this coast. The city was
celebrating
the annual feast of Neptune; during it
Lysimachus saw the Tyrian ship,
with its black banners, with rich trimmings;
and he rushes there eagerly in his barge.
Now imagine once again unhappy Pericles,
and think this stage is his ship,
where the action will show us what happened,
and more may be revealed; please sit and listen.*

Exit

Enter two Sailors, one belonging to the Tyrian vessel, the other to the barge; to them HELICANUS

Tyrian Sailor

[To the Sailor of Mytilene] Where is lord Helicanus?
he can resolve you.
O, here he is.
Sir, there's a barge put off from Mytilene,
And in it is Lysimachus the governor,
Who craves to come aboard. What is your will?

Where is Lord Helicanus?
He can answer your question.
Oh, here he is.
Sir, a barge has sailed out from Mytilene,
and in it is Lysimachus the governor,
who asks permission to come aboard. What do
you want to do?

HELICANUS
That he have his. Call up some gentlemen.

What he wants to do. Summon some gentlemen.

Tyrian Sailor
Ho, gentlemen! my lord calls.

Hello there, gentlemen! My lord calls you.

Enter two or three Gentlemen

First Gentleman
Doth your lordship call?

Did your lordship call?

HELICANUS
Gentlemen, there's some of worth would come aboard;

Gentlemen, there are some dignitaries who want
to come aboard;

I pray ye, greet them fairly.

please go and give them a warm welcome.

The Gentlemen and the two Sailors descend, and go on board the barge

Enter, from thence, LYSIMACHUS and Lords; with the Gentlemen and the two Sailors

Tyrian Sailor
Sir,
This is the man that can, in aught you would,
Resolve you.

Sir,
this is the man who can answer
any questions you have.

LYSIMACHUS
Hail, reverend sir! the gods preserve you!

Greetings, honourable gentleman! May be gods
preserve you!

HELICANUS
And you, sir, to outlive the age I am,
And die as I would do.

And you, sir, to live to be older than I am,
and to die as I hope to.

LYSIMACHUS
You wish me well.
Being on shore, honouring of Neptune's triumphs,
Seeing this goodly vessel ride before us,
I made to it, to know of whence you are.

That is a kind wish.
I was on shore, celebrating the feast of Neptune,
when I saw this handsome ship come into view,
so I made for it, to know where you have come
from.

HELICANUS
First, what is your place?

Firstly, what is your position?

LYSIMACHUS
I am the governor of this place you lie before.

I am the governor of this place where you have anchored.

HELICANUS
Sir,
Our vessel is of Tyre, in it the king;
A man who for this three months hath not spoken
To any one, nor taken sustenance
But to prorogue his grief.

Sir,
our ship comes from Tyre, containing the king;
a man who has not spoken to anyone for
the last three months, nor eaten anything
except what is sufficient to keep him alive to
grieve.

LYSIMACHUS
Upon what ground is his distemperature?

What's the reason for his depression?

HELICANUS
'Twould be too tedious to repeat;
But the main grief springs from the loss
Of a beloved daughter and a wife.

It would take too long to explain;
but his chief sorrow comes from the loss
of a beloved daughter and wife.

LYSIMACHUS
May we not see him?

Can't we see him?

HELICANUS
You may;
But bootless is your sight: he will not speak to any.

You may;
but there will be no point to it: he won't speak to
anyone.

LYSIMACHUS
Yet let me obtain my wish.

Still, let me have my wish.

HELICANUS
Behold him.

Look at him.

PERICLES discovered
This was a goodly person,
Till the disaster that, one mortal night,
Drove him to this.

This was a fine man,
until the disaster that, one fateful night,
turned him into this.

LYSIMACHUS
Sir king, all hail! the gods preserve you!

Hail, royal sir!

Sir king, all welcome! May the gods preserve
you!
Greetings, royal sir!

HELICANUS
It is in vain; he will not speak to you.

There is no point; he won't speak to you.

First Lord
Sir,
We have a maid in Mytilene, I durst wager,

Would win some words of him.

Sir,
there's a girl in Mytilene who, I'd be prepared to bet,
could persuade him to talk.

LYSIMACHUS
'Tis well bethought.
She questionless with her sweet harmony
And other chosen attractions, would allure,
And make a battery through his deafen'd parts,
Which now are midway stopp'd:
She is all happy as the fairest of all,
And, with her fellow maids is now upon
The leafy shelter that abuts against
The island's side.

Good thinking.
Without question her sweet harmonies,
and other great attractions, could charm him,
and win through his deaf ears,
which are now blocked:
she is as wonderful as a goddess,
and with her girlfriends she is now
in the leafy grove which abuts
the side of the island.

Whispers a Lord, who goes off in the barge of LYSIMACHUS

HELICANUS
Sure, all's effectless; yet nothing we'll omit

That bears recovery's name. But, since your kindness
We have stretch'd thus far, let us beseech you
That for our gold we may provision have,
Wherein we are not destitute for want,
But weary for the staleness.

It's certain that nothing will work; but we'll try anything
that looks like a cure. But, as you have been
so kind thus far, please can we ask you
to sell us some provisions;
we don't lack for quantity,
but we are tired of their quality.

LYSIMACHUS
O, sir, a courtesy
Which if we should deny, the most just gods
For every graff would send a caterpillar,
And so afflict our province. Yet once more
Let me entreat to know at large the cause
Of your king's sorrow.

Oh, sir, if we were to deny
you such a courtesy, the most just gods
would send a caterpillar to every plant
to plague our province. But once again
let me beg you to tell me more details
of the cause of your king's sorrow.

HELICANUS
Sit, sir, I will recount it to you:
But, see, I am prevented.

Sit down, sir, I will tell you about it:
but, you see, this interrupts me.

Re-enter, from the barge, Lord, with MARINA, and a young Lady

LYSIMACHUS
O, here is

Oh, here is

The lady that I sent for. Welcome, fair one!
Is't not a goodly presence?

the lady that I sent for. Welcome, beautiful one!
Isn't she wonderful?

HELICANUS
She's a gallant lady.

She's a noble lady.

LYSIMACHUS
She's such a one, that, were I well assured
Came of a gentle kind and noble stock,

She is such a one that If I could be certain
that she came from a gentle, kind and noble
family,

I'ld wish no better choice, and think me rarely wed.

I would wish to have no better, and would think
I had made a fine marriage.

Fair one, all goodness that consists in bounty

Beautiful one, you can expect all the best
rewards

Expect even here, where is a kingly patient:
If that thy prosperous and artificial feat

even here, where the patient is a king:
if all your wonderful and skilful
accomplishments

Can draw him but to answer thee in aught,
Thy sacred physic shall receive such pay
As thy desires can wish.

can just get him to say anything to you,
your blessed treatment will be paid for
with anything you desire.

MARINA
Sir, I will use
My utmost skill in his recovery, provided
That none but I and my companion maid
Be suffer'd to come near him.

Sir, I will do
everything I can to help him, provided
that nobody but I and my friend here
are allowed to come near him.

LYSIMACHUS
Come, let us leave her;
And the gods make her prosperous!

Come, let us leave her;
and may the gods give her success!

MARINA sings

LYSIMACHUS
Mark'd he your music?

Did he take any notice of your music?

MARINA
No, nor look'd on us.

No, and he didn't look at us.

LYSIMACHUS
See, she will speak to him.

See, she will speak to him.

MARINA
Hail, sir! my lord, lend ear.

Greetings, sir! My Lord, listen to me.

PERICLES
Hum, ha!

Hmm, ha!

MARINA
I am a maid,
My lord, that ne'er before invited eyes,

But have been gazed on like a comet: she speaks,

My lord, that, may be, hath endured a grief
Might equal yours, if both were justly weigh'd.

Though wayward fortune did malign my state,
My derivation was from ancestors
Who stood equivalent with mighty kings:
But time hath rooted out my parentage,

And to the world and awkward casualties
Bound me in servitude.

Aside
I will desist;
But there is something glows upon my cheek,
And whispers in mine ear, 'Go not till he speak.'

PERICLES
My fortunes--parentage--good parentage--
To equal mine!--was it not thus? what say you?

MARINA
I said, my lord, if you did know my parentage,
You would not do me violence.

PERICLES
I do think so. Pray you, turn your eyes upon me.
You are like something that--What country-woman?

Here of these shores?

MARINA
No, nor of any shores:
Yet I was mortally brought forth, and am
No other than I appear.

PERICLES
I am great with woe, and shall deliver weeping.
My dearest wife was like this maid, and such a one
My daughter might have been: my queen's square brows;
Her stature to an inch; as wand-like straight;

I am a girl,
my Lord, who never before asked anyone to look at me,
but have been stared at as if I was a comet: the one who speaks
to you, my lord, has suffered from sorrows which might be the equal of yours, if they were fairly compared.
Though changeable fortune brought me low,
I am descended from ancestors who were the equals of mighty kings; but time has stripped me of my ancestry, and made me
the plaything of the world and its accidents.

I will stop;
but there is something inside me which says I should not leave until he speaks.

My fortunes--parentage--good parentage--
the equal of mine!--Wasn't that it? What did you say?

I said, my lord, if you knew my ancestry, you would not push me away.

I think so. Please, look at me.
You are something like that--what country are you from, woman?
Do you come from these shores?

No, nor from any shores:
and yet I had a mortal birth, and I am nothing more than I seem to be.

I am full of sorrow, and will let it out in tears.
My dearest wife was like this girl, she could be my daughter: she has my queen's square brow; exactly the same height; just as perfectly straight;

As silver-voiced; her eyes as jewel-like
And cased as richly; in pace another Juno;

Who starves the ears she feeds, and makes them hungry,

The more she gives them speech. Where do you live?

*just as silver voiced; her eyes are as jewel like
and in the same rich setting; her carriage like a
goddess;
she starves the ears she feeds, the more she
speaks
to them, the more they want to hear. Where do
you live?*

MARINA
Where I am but a stranger: from the deck

You may discern the place.

*Where I am just a foreigner: you can see the
place
from the deck.*

PERICLES
Where were you bred?
And how achieved you these endowments, which
You make more rich to owe?

*Where were you brought up?
How did you gain these accomplishments, which
are even richer because they are yours?*

MARINA
If I should tell my history, it would seem
Like lies disdain'd in the reporting.

*If I told you my story, it would seem like
lies which would be disbelieved even as I spoke
them.*

PERICLES
Prithee, speak:
Falseness cannot come from thee; for thou look'st
Modest as Justice, and thou seem'st a palace
For the crown'd Truth to dwell in: I will
believe thee,
And make my senses credit thy relation
To points that seem impossible; for thou look'st
Like one I loved indeed. What were thy friends?

Didst thou not say, when I did push thee back--
Which was when I perceived thee--that thou camest
From good descending?

*Please, speak:
you would not be capable of lies; you look
as modest as justice, and you are like a palace
where the king of truth would live: I will
believe you,
and I will allow myself to believe your story
however impossible it seems; for you look
like someone I loved very dearly. Who were your
family?
Didn't you say when I pushed you away,
which was when I noticed you, that you came
from a good family?*

MARINA
So indeed I did.

I did indeed.

PERICLES
Report thy parentage. I think thou said'st
Thou hadst been toss'd from wrong to injury,
And that thou thought'st thy griefs might equal mine,

If both were open'd.

*Tell me of your ancestry. I think you said
that you had been thrown from bad to worse,
and that you thought your grief might equal
mine,
if they were compared.*

MARINA

Some such thing
I said, and said no more but what my thoughts
Did warrant me was likely.

*I said something
like that, and I was only saying what I thought
was probably the case.*

PERICLES
Tell thy story;
If thine consider'd prove the thousandth part
Of my endurance, thou art a man, and I
Have suffer'd like a girl: yet thou dost look
Like Patience gazing on kings' graves, and smiling

*Tell me your story;
if your sufferings are one thousandth of mine
then you are a man, and I
have suffered like a girl: and yet you look
like the statues of Patience gazing on the graves
of kings,*

Extremity out of act. What were thy friends?

*making the worst things melt away with your
smile. What was your family?*

How lost thou them? Thy name, my most kind virgin?

*How did you lose them? What is your name,
my sweet girl?*

Recount, I do beseech thee: come, sit by me.

Tell me, I beg you: come and sit down by me.

MARINA
My name is Marina.

My name is Marina.

PERICLES
O, I am mock'd,
And thou by some incensed god sent hither
To make the world to laugh at me.

*Oh, I am mocked,
and some angry God has sent you here
to make the world laugh at me.*

MARINA
Patience, good sir,
Or here I'll cease.

*Be calm, good sir,
or I won't speak.*

PERICLES
Nay, I'll be patient.
Thou little know'st how thou dost startle me,
To call thyself Marina.

*I will be calm.
You have no idea how much you startled me,
calling yourself Marina.*

MARINA
The name
Was given me by one that had some power,
My father, and a king.

*The name
was given to me by a powerful man,
my father, who was a king.*

PERICLES
How! a king's daughter?
And call'd Marina?

*What's that! A king's daughter?
And called Marina?*

MARINA
You said you would believe me;
But, not to be a troubler of your peace,
I will end here.

*You said that you would believe me;
but I won't disturb your peace any more,
I'll stop here.*

PERICLES
But are you flesh and blood?
Have you a working pulse? and are no fairy?
Motion! Well; speak on. Where were you born?

And wherefore call'd Marina?

MARINA
Call'd Marina
For I was born at sea.

PERICLES
At sea! what mother?

MARINA
My mother was the daughter of a king;
Who died the minute I was born,
As my good nurse Lychorida hath oft
Deliver'd weeping.

PERICLES
O, stop there a little!

Aside
This is the rarest dream that e'er dull sleep
Did mock sad fools withal: this cannot be:
My daughter's buried. Well: where were you bred?

I'll hear you more, to the bottom of your story,
And never interrupt you.

MARINA
You scorn: believe me, 'twere best I did give o'er.

PERICLES
I will believe you by the syllable
Of what you shall deliver. Yet, give me leave:
How came you in these parts? where were you bred?

MARINA
The king my father did in Tarsus leave me;
Till cruel Cleon, with his wicked wife,
Did seek to murder me: and having woo'd
A villain to attempt it, who having drawn to do't,

A crew of pirates came and rescued me;

But are you flesh and blood?
Do you have a pulse? You are not a spirit?
You are not a statue! Good; speak on. Where
were you born?
And why are you called Marina?

I was called Marina
because I was born at sea.

At sea! Who was your mother?

My mother was the daughter of the King;
she died in childbirth,
as my good nurse Lychordia had often
tearfully told me.

Oh, just pause for a moment!

This is the strangest dream that stupid sleep
ever used to mock sad fools: this cannot be:
my daughter is in her grave. Well: where were
you brought up?
I want to hear more, right to the end,
and I won't interrupt you.

You don't believe me: it would be best for me to
stop.

I shall believe you through hearing
what you have to say. But, excuse me:
how did you come to these parts? Where were
you brought up?

The king, my father, left me in Tarsus;
until cruel Cleon, with his wicked wife,
tried to murder me: they had persuaded
a villain to try it, and he had already drawn his
sword
when a crew of pirates came and rescued me;

Brought me to Mytilene. But, good sir,
Whither will you have me? Why do you weep?
It may be,
You think me an impostor: no, good faith;
I am the daughter to King Pericles,
If good King Pericles be.

they brought me to Mytilene. But, good sir,
what do you want from me? Why do you weep?
It may be,
that you think I am an impostor: I swear I'm not;
I am the daughter of King Pericles,
if good King Pericles still lives.

PERICLES
Ho, Helicanus!

Helicanus, come here!

HELICANUS
Calls my lord?

You called, my lord?

PERICLES
Thou art a grave and noble counsellor,
Most wise in general: tell me, if thou canst,

What this maid is, or what is like to be,
That thus hath made me weep?

You are a serious and noble counsellor,
with great wisdom in all things: tell me, if you
can,
who this girl is, or what she may be,
that has made me weep like this.

HELICANUS
I know not; but
Here is the regent, sir, of Mytilene
Speaks nobly of her.

I do not know; but
here is the regent, sir, of Mytilene
who speaks very well of her.

LYSIMACHUS
She would never tell
Her parentage; being demanded that,
She would sit still and weep.

She would never say
who her parents were; when she was asked,
she would sit down and weep.

PERICLES
O Helicanus, strike me, honour'd sir;
Give me a gash, put me to present pain;
Lest this great sea of joys rushing upon me
O'erbear the shores of my mortality,
And drown me with their sweetness. O, come hither,

Thou that beget'st him that did thee beget;

Thou that wast born at sea, buried at Tarsus,
And found at sea again! O Helicanus,
Down on thy knees, thank the holy gods as loud

As thunder threatens us: this is Marina.
What was thy mother's name? tell me but that,

For truth can never be confirm'd enough,
Though doubts did ever sleep.

Oh Helicanus, strike me, honoured sir;
cut me, give me a pain to take my mind off
this great sea of joy which is rushing over me,
in case it should swamp the shores of my life,
and drown me with its sweetness. Oh, come
here,
you who have given new life to the one who
gave you life;
you who was born at sea, buried at Tarsus,
and found at sea again! Oh Helicanus,
get down on your knees! Thank the holy gods
as loud
as thunder: this is Marina.
What was your mother's name? If you can just
tell me that,
for there can never be enough proof of truth,
even when there is no doubt.

MARINA
First, sir, I pray,
What is your title?

First, sir, I must ask you,
what is your title?

PERICLES
I am Pericles of Tyre: but tell me now
My drown'd queen's name, as in the rest you said

Thou hast been godlike perfect,
The heir of kingdoms and another like
To Pericles thy father.

I am Pericles of Tyre: but now tell me
the name of my drowned queen, as everything
else you've said
has been divinely perfect, showing you
to be the heir of kingdoms and of the same blood
as Pericles your father.

MARINA
Is it no more to be your daughter than
To say my mother's name was Thaisa?
Thaisa was my mother, who did end
The minute I began.

Is all I have to do to be your daughter
to say that my mother's name was Thaisa?
Thaisa was my mother, who died
the minute I came to life.

PERICLES
Now, blessing on thee! rise; thou art my child.

Give me fresh garments. Mine own, Helicanus;

She is not dead at Tarsus, as she should have been,

By savage Cleon: she shall tell thee all;

When thou shalt kneel, and justify in knowledge
She is thy very princess. Who is this?

Now, blessings upon you! Rise; you are my
child.
Bring me fresh clothes. This is my child,
Helicanus;
she was not killed at Tarsus, as she should have
been,
by the wicked Cleon: she will tell you
everything;
then you shall kneel, satisfied in the knowledge
that she is truly your princess. Who is this?

HELICANUS
Sir, 'tis the governor of Mytilene,
Who, hearing of your melancholy state,
Did come to see you.

Sir, this is the governor of Mytilene,
who, hearing of your melancholy state,
came to see you.

PERICLES
I embrace you.
Give me my robes. I am wild in my beholding.

O heavens bless my girl! But, hark, what music?

Tell Helicanus, my Marina, tell him
O'er, point by point, for yet he seems to doubt,
How sure you are my daughter. But, what music?

I embrace you.
Give me my robes. I'm almost mad with what
I see.
O heavens bless my girl! But, listen, what's
that music?
Tell Helicanus, my Marina, tell him
again, point by point, for he still seems to doubt
that you are definitely my daughter. But, what is
that music?

HELICANUS

My lord, I hear none.

My Lord, I can hear none.

PERICLES
None!
The music of the spheres! List, my Marina.

None!
It's the music of the stars! Listen, my Marina.

LYSIMACHUS
It is not good to cross him; give him way.

It's not good to contradict him; let him run on.

PERICLES
Rarest sounds! Do ye not hear?

Amazing sounds! Can't you hear it?

LYSIMACHUS
My lord, I hear.

My Lord, I hear it.

Music

PERICLES
Most heavenly music!
It nips me unto listening, and thick slumber
Hangs upon mine eyes: let me rest.

Most heavenly music!
It forces me to listen, and heavy sleep
weighs down my eyelids: let me rest.

Sleeps

LYSIMACHUS
A pillow for his head:
So, leave him all. Well, my companion friends,
If this but answer to my just belief,
I'll well remember you.

Put a pillow under his head:
so, let's all leave him. Well, my dear friends,
if all this is as true as I think,
you will be well rewarded.

Exeunt all but PERICLES

DIANA appears to PERICLES as in a vision

DIANA
My temple stands in Ephesus: hie thee thither,
And do upon mine altar sacrifice.
There, when my maiden priests are met together,

My temple stands in Ephesus: go there,
and make a sacrifice at my altar.
There, when my virgin priests are gathered
together,

Before the people all,
Reveal how thou at sea didst lose thy wife:
To mourn thy crosses, with thy daughter's, call

in front of all the people,
reveal how you lost your wife at sea:
to mourn your misfortunes, with your
daughter's,

And give them repetition to the life.
Or perform my bidding, or thou livest in woe;
Do it, and happy; by my silver bow!
Awake, and tell thy dream.

repeat them all, word for word.
Do as I say, or you will live in sorrow;
do it and you will be happy; by my silver bow!
Wake up, and tell people your dream.

Disappears

PERICLES
Celestial Dian, goddess argentine,
I will obey thee. Helicanus!

Heavenly Diana, silver goddess,
I shall obey you. Helicanus!

Re-enter HELICANUS, LYSIMACHUS, and MARINA

HELICANUS
Sir?

Sir?

PERICLES
My purpose was for Tarsus, there to strike
The inhospitable Cleon; but I am
For other service first: toward Ephesus
Turn our blown sails; eftsoons I'll tell thee why.

I meant to make for Tarsus, to attack
the evil Cleon; but I have
another job to do first; turn the ships
towards Ephesus; soon I'll tell you why.

To LYSIMACHUS
Shall we refresh us, sir, upon your shore,
And give you gold for such provision
As our intents will need?

Shall we take refreshment, sir, upon your shore,
and pay you for the provisions
we shall need for our plans?

LYSIMACHUS
Sir,
With all my heart; and, when you come ashore,
I have another suit.

Sir,
with all my heart; and, when you come ashore,
I have something to ask you.

PERICLES
You shall prevail,
Were it to woo my daughter; for it seems
You have been noble towards her.

If you want permission to woo my daughter
you shall succeed; for it seems
you have treated her nobly.

LYSIMACHUS
Sir, lend me your arm.

Sir, give me your arm.

PERICLES
Come, my Marina.

Come, my Marina.

Exeunt

SCENE II:

Enter GOWER, before the temple of DIANA at Ephesus

GOWER
Now our sands are almost run;
More a little, and then dumb.
This, my last boon, give me,
For such kindness must relieve me,
That you aptly will suppose
What pageantry, what feats, what shows,
What minstrelsy, and pretty din,
The regent made in Mytilene
To greet the king. So he thrived,
That he is promised to be wived
To fair Marina; but in no wise
Till he had done his sacrifice,
As Dian bade: whereto being bound,
The interim, pray you, all confound.
In feather'd briefness sails are fill'd,
And wishes fall out as they're will'd.
At Ephesus, the temple see,
Our king and all his company.
That he can hither come so soon,
Is by your fancy's thankful doom.

Exit

Now our time is almost up;
a little more and then we'll be silent.
Please indulge me one more time,
be kind enough
to imagine
the pageantry, the exploits, the shows,
the songs, and happy music,
the regent ordered in Mytilene
to welcome the king. He had the fortune
to gain the promise that he should marry
fair Marina, although certainly not
until the sacrifice has been made
as Diana ordered: they are going there,
so please forget the interim.
The sails hoisted and are speeding,
and wishes will come to pass.
At Ephesus you can see the temple
and our king and all his company.
That he can get there so quickly
is thanks to your imaginations.

SCENE III. The temple of Diana at Ephesus; THAISA standing

near the altar, as high priestess; a number of
Virgins on each side; CERIMON and other Inhabitants
of Ephesus attending.

Enter PERICLES, with his train; LYSIMACHUS, HELICANUS, MARINA, and a Lady

PERICLES
Hail, Dian! to perform thy just command,
I here confess myself the king of Tyre;
Who, frighted from my country, did wed
At Pentapolis the fair Thaisa.
At sea in childbed died she, but brought forth
A maid-child call'd Marina; who, O goddess,
Wears yet thy silver livery. She at Tarsus
Was nursed with Cleon; who at fourteen years

He sought to murder: but her better stars
Brought her to Mytilene; 'gainst whose shore
Riding, her fortunes brought the maid aboard us,

Where, by her own most clear remembrance, she
Made known herself my daughter.

THAISA
Voice and favour!
You are, you are--O royal Pericles!

Faints

PERICLES
What means the nun? she dies! help, gentlemen!

CERIMON
Noble sir,
If you have told Diana's altar true,
This is your wife.

PERICLES
Reverend appearer, no;
I threw her overboard with these very arms.

CERIMON
Upon this coast, I warrant you.

PERICLES
'Tis most certain.

CERIMON
Look to the lady; O, she's but o'erjoy'd.

Early in blustering morn this lady was

Hail to you, Diana! To do as you have ordered,
I here reveal myself as king of Tyre;
who, fled from my country, married
the beautiful Thaisa at Pentapolis.
She died in childbirth at sea, but delivered
a girl child called Murina; who, oh goddess,
is still one of your virgins. She was brought up
at Tarsus by Cleon; when she was fourteen years
old he tried to murder her; but her lucky stars
brought her to Mytilene; when we arrived
at those shores, fate brought the girl onto my ship,
where, with the aid of her clear memories, she
proved herself to be my daughter.

Voice and face!
It's you, it's you–oh royal Pericles!

What does the nun mean? She's dying! Help,
gentlemen!

Noble sir,
if you have told the truth at Diana's altar,
this is your wife.

Reverend stranger, no;
I threw her overboard with these very arms.

In this sea, I am sure.

Certainly.

Take care of the lady; oh, she's only overcome
with joy.
Early on a stormy morning this lady was

Thrown upon this shore. I oped the coffin,
Found there rich jewels; recover'd her, and placed her

Here in Diana's temple.

PERICLES
May we see them?

CERIMON
Great sir, they shall be brought you to my house,

Whither I invite you. Look, Thaisa is recovered.

THAISA
O, let me look!
If he be none of mine, my sanctity
Will to my sense bend no licentious ear,
But curb it, spite of seeing. O, my lord,
Are you not Pericles? Like him you spake,
Like him you are: did you not name a tempest,
A birth, and death?

PERICLES
The voice of dead Thaisa!

THAISA
That Thaisa am I, supposed dead
And drown'd.

PERICLES
Immortal Dian!

THAISA
Now I know you better.
When we with tears parted Pentapolis,
The king my father gave you such a ring.

Points to Pericles' ring

PERICLES
This, this: no more, you gods! your present kindness

Makes my past miseries sports: you shall do well,

That on the touching of her lips I may
Melt and no more be seen. O, come, be buried
A second time within these arms.

114

*cast up upon this shore. I opened the coffin,
and found rich jewels inside; I brought her back
to life, and placed her
here in Diana's temple.*

May we see them?

*Great sir, they shall be brought to you at my
house,
which I invite you to. Look, Thaisa has
recovered.*

*Oh, let me look!
If he is not mine, my holiness
will not allow me to believe it
in spite of the evidence of my eyes. Oh, my lord,
are you not Pericles? You spoke like him,
you look like him: did you not speak of a storm,
a birth, and a death?*

This is the voice of dead Thaisa!

*I am that Thaisa, thought to be dead
and drowned.*

Immortal Diana!

*Now I know you better.
When we left Pentapolis in tears,
my father the king gave you a ring like that.*

*It is, it is: no more, you gods! Your current
kindness
makes my previous miseries seem nothing: it
would be fitting
for me, when I touch her lips, to melt away
and never be seen again. Oh, come, and have
a second burial within these arms.*

MARINA
My heart
Leaps to be gone into my mother's bosom.

Kneels to THAISA

PERICLES
Look, who kneels here! Flesh of thy flesh, Thaisa;

Thy burden at the sea, and call'd Marina

For she was yielded there.

THAISA
Blest, and mine own!

HELICANUS
Hail, madam, and my queen!

THAISA
I know you not.

PERICLES
You have heard me say, when I did fly from Tyre,

I left behind an ancient substitute:
Can you remember what I call'd the man?
I have named him oft.

THAISA
'Twas Helicanus then.

PERICLES
Still confirmation:
Embrace him, dear Thaisa; this is he.
Now do I long to hear how you were found;
How possibly preserved; and who to thank,

Besides the gods, for this great miracle.

THAISA
Lord Cerimon, my lord; this man,
Through whom the gods have shown their power; that
Can
From first to last resolve you.

My heart
leaps to have found my mother again.

Look who is kneeling here! Your own flesh
and blood, Thaisa;
the one you delivered at sea, who was called
Marina
after the place of her birth.

Blessed, and my own!

I salute you, my lady and my queen!

I don't know you.

You have heard me say, that when I fled from
Tyre,
I left behind an old man in my place:
can you remember what I called the man?
I often mentioned him.

You called him Helicanus.

Even more proof:
embrace him, dear Thaisa; this is him.
Now I long to hear how you were found;
how on earth you survived; and who I have to
thank,
apart from the gods, for this great miracle.

Lord Cerimon, my lord; this man,
through whom the gods have shown their power;

he's the one who can explain things to you from
start to finish.

PERICLES
Reverend sir,
The gods can have no mortal officer
More like a god than you. Will you deliver

How this dead queen re-lives?

Holy Sir,
there can be no human servant of the gods
who is more like a god than you. Can you
explain
how this dead queen was brought back to life?

CERIMON
I will, my lord.
Beseech you, first go with me to my house,
Where shall be shown you all was found with her;

How she came placed here in the temple;

No needful thing omitted.

I will, my lord.
Please, first come with me to my house,
where you will be shown all the things that were
found with her;
I'll explain why she came to be here in the
temple;
I won't omit a single detail.

PERICLES
Pure Dian, bless thee for thy vision! I
Will offer night-oblations to thee. Thaisa,
This prince, the fair-betrothed of your daughter,
Shall marry her at Pentapolis. And now,
This ornament
Makes me look dismal will I clip to form;
And what this fourteen years no razor touch'd,
To grace thy marriage-day, I'll beautify.

Pure Diana, bless you for your vision! I
will offer up my prayers to you. Thaisa,
this prince, the good fiance of your daughter,
shall marry her at Pentapolis. And now,
I shall clip this decoration, which
makes me look so miserable, into shape;
to honour your wedding day, I'll dress
that which no razor has touched for fourteen
years.

THAISA
Lord Cerimon hath letters of good credit, sir,
My father's dead.

Lord Cerimon has credible information, sir,
that my father is dead.

PERICLES
Heavens make a star of him! Yet there, my queen,

We'll celebrate their nuptials, and ourselves

Will in that kingdom spend our following days:
Our son and daughter shall in Tyrus reign.
Lord Cerimon, we do our longing stay
To hear the rest untold: sir, lead's the way.

May the heavens welcome him! But there, my
queen,
we shall celebrate their wedding, and we
ourselves
will live out our days in that kingdom:
our son and daughter will reign in Tyre.
Lord Cerimon, I will suspend for a short while
my longing to hear the rest of the story: sir, lead
the way.

Exeunt

Enter GOWER

GOWER
In Antiochus and his daughter you have heard

In Antiochus and his daughter you have heard

116

Of monstrous lust the due and just reward:

In Pericles, his queen and daughter, seen,

Although assail'd with fortune fierce and keen,
Virtue preserved from fell destruction's blast,
Led on by heaven, and crown'd with joy at last:
In Helicanus may you well descry
A figure of truth, of faith, of loyalty:
In reverend Cerimon there well appears
The worth that learned charity aye wears:
For wicked Cleon and his wife, when fame
Had spread their cursed deed, and honour'd name

Of Pericles, to rage the city turn,
That him and his they in his palace burn;

The gods for murder seemed so content
To punish them; although not done, but meant.

So, on your patience evermore attending,
New joy wait on you! Here our play has ending.

Exit

of how monstrous lust got its right and proper reward:
in Pericles, his queen and daughter, you have seen,
although attacked by terrible fate,
virtue saved from the awful blast of destruction,
led on by heaven, and crowned with joy at last:
in Helicanus you can certainly see
an example of truth, of faith and loyalty:
in holy Cerimon there is a good example
of the virtues of wise charity.
For wicked Cleon and his wife, when it became known of his terrible assault on the honoured name
of Pericles, the city turned to rage,
and they burned him and his family in his palace:
the gods seemed happy with this punishment for murder; although it was not done, it was intended.
So for your patience in listening to us,
May we wish you happiness! This is the end of our play.

117

Printed in Great Britain
by Amazon